WELBORN
17503 Marine Drive, Stanwood, WA 98292

WHITEWATER MAILMEN

THE STORY OF THE ROGUE RIVER MAIL BOATS

By
Gary & Gloria Meier

— A Maverick Publication —

ISBN 0-89288-216-6

Library of Congress Catalogue Card Number 91-60926

Maverick Publications, Inc.
P. O. Box 5007 • Bend, Oregon 97708

Table Of Contents

Lex Fromm

1949

1990

Dedication

We were riding the Rogue River with a legend. He sat bundled against the chill in the open mail boat, his eyes riveted by long habit to each riffle and rapid; reading currents, judging channels. He was not piloting the boat, though he could have, for he has been on intimate terms with the Rogue, in all her moods, for over seven decades. He was along as a passenger that day, reliving past adventures and sharing stories about an earlier time on the famous river that has been so much a part of his life. At times he was quiet, inwardly reflecting on memories only he will ever know. Local fishermen we passed recognized him and waved. The word quickly spread that the "King of the Rogue" was on the river.

For almost twenty years, from 1946 to 1964, he and partners operated the Rogue River Mail Boats. And in high water or low, he always got the mail through. He and his mail boats were a lifeline for those who lived in the remote reaches of the Rogue River Canyon. Through his daring rescues and helping hands, this kind and generous man has given much more to the river and her people than he has taken.

He was a respected educator of children, sought-after fishing guide, and popular champion of the Southern Oregon Coast and its scenic attractions. And, at 81, he still enjoys a wide reputation as an innovative, expert builder of hand-crafted boats.

To Lex Fromm, the premier boatman of the lower Rogue River, this book is respectfully dedicated.

And the river glided on in endless solitude,
its eternal song, low and musical, near at hand,
droning sweet melody from the rapid at the bend,
and filling the distant drowsy air with its soft thunder.

Zane Grey in
Rogue River Feud

Acknowledgments

It is always a pleasure, when the book writing is done, to reflect on the folks who helped us over the trail. We think of ourselves as mere "court scribes," capturing on paper the words and deeds of others, and as such we needed the way pointed by knowledgeable people, guidance by those whose lives have been and are tightly interwoven with the Rogue River and the mail boats. They know the subject better than we ever will. They were the teachers, we the students.

Foremost, we would like to thank Lex Fromm, DeForest Sorber, and Abe Fry, true gentlemen of the Rogue River, who shared memories and stories, and who graciously answered questions about the way things were.

We are also grateful to the mail boat pilots, past and present, who courteously gave us their stories and anecdotes, and explained in detail what they do and why they do it. We especially thank: Scott Adams, Tim Arntzen, Gary Combs, Jon Hockema, Hugh McGinnis, Gordon Smithers, Jim Sorber, Dennis "Mutt" Wade, and Stan Wade. And thanks to Laurie Wills and Charlotte DeLore for stories about their father, Bruce Bobo. Thanks also to the upriver people who went out of their way to help us with recollections and old photographs, particularly: Bob and Monica Doerr, Carolyn Rutledge, Chris (Edgerton) Ahlstrom, Bernard and Clarice Jackson of Cougar Lane Lodge, the Scherbarths (Bill, Julie, John, and Gemma) of Singing Springs Ranch, Willard Lucas of Lucas Pioneer Ranch, Larry and Clare Bowen of Clay Hill Lodge, and Ernie and Violet Rutledge of Illahe Lodge.

We also thank Cynthia Kuhlman, Rebecca Soward-Hawman, Bob Alexander, Larry McLane, Beverly (Price) Cooney, Beverly Sokol, Molly Walker of the *Curry County Reporter*, Agness Postmaster Sandy Stallard, Janene Paul at the Coos-Curry Electric Cooperative, Steven Lorton, Northwest editor of *Sunset* magazine, the competent and courteous staffs of the Curry County Historical Society, and the University of Oregon Library, Oregon Collection and Microfilm Department.

Finally, we want to express special gratitude to Ed and Sue Kammer, present owners of Rogue River Mail Boat Trips, without whose help and friendship this book literally could not have been written.

We are grateful to all of you. This is your book as much as ours.

The Authors

Foreword

One of the oldest and most popular traditions on the Oregon Coast began in 1895 on the Rogue River. It was born humbly, arising out of the need of remote settlers and miners living in the vast wilderness of the Rogue River Canyon to communicate with the outside world, to send and receive letters and packages to and from distant relatives, to stay associated with friends far away. From this need to communicate, intensified by isolation, evolved a tenacious human enterprise, struggling to overcome forces of nature in a whitewater world. The history of that achievement is a chronicle of dedication and vision and heroism, punctuated by tragedy, accented with humor. It is a tradition that has endured and grown into one of the most unique and famous visitor attractions in the West.

This is the story of the Rogue River Mail Boats.

• • •

Each year thousands of people ride the exciting blue mail boats far up the Rogue River to enjoy the scenic wonders and wildlife in one of America's supreme beauty spots. The famous 64-, 80-, and 104-mile trips up the riffles and rapids of the Rogue have been well-documented in the nation's press and magazines. But little has ever been written about the fascinating, dramatic history of the mail boats; few articles and no full-length books.

Researching this interesting subject was pleasant work for us, both having taken our first mail boat rides as youngsters in the early 1950s. Our chief reliance was on primary sources, such as old-time mail boatmen Lex Fromm, Abe Fry, DeForest Sorber, and Dennis "Mutt" Wade, who shared stories and recollections of how it was in days long gone. We also found considerable mail boat history in the newspapers of the day. Over 450 hours were spent reviewing microfilmed newspapers in the University of Oregon. We also obtained mail boat records and contracts from the musty confines of that great repository of America's paperwork, the National Archives.

Helpful, too, were sons and daughters of deceased mail boatmen and river lodge owners, who kindly gave us family information and details concerning the value of the mail boats to upriver life in the early years of this century. We also talked to veteran river residents who have lived in the Rogue Canyon for fifty and more years, who searched memories, scrapbooks, and photograph albums for anecdotes and pictures of mail boats in the 1930s, '40s, and '50s.

The result of that research is what you now hold in your hands. The history of the Rogue River mail boats has been an exciting journey of human achievement. We hope this book will pass that excitement on to you.

Gary & Gloria Meier
Eugene, Oregon

CHAPTER 1

A River Called Rogue

Oregon's famed Rogue River is born as a gushing stream high in the Cascade Range, 215 miles from the sea. It comes bubbling from massive, icy Boundary Springs in the northwest corner of Crater Lake National Park, at the foot of Mount Mazama, the extinct volcano that holds Crater Lake. Fed by Mazama Creek, Cascade Creek, National Creek, and numerous other mountain streams and springs, the Rogue quickly gathers size as it dashes and tumbles south down the slopes of the Cascades. Soon it is joined by its Middle and South Forks at Lost Creek Reservoir, built to help restrain wild winter rampages.

The river eventually turns west and flows through its namesake valley, past Medford and Grants Pass and the confluence with one of its two principal tributaries, the Applegate River.

Headwaters of the Rogue River near Crater Lake.
(Oregon State Highway Division Photo)

It was in this area, between the present city of Grants Pass and the mouth of the Applegate, that the Rogue River was named. Fifteen brigades of French-Canadian fur trappers, in the employ of Hudson's Bay Company, crossed the river here from 1825 to 1843. They called the large, swift stream *La Riviere Aux Coquins* (The River of the Rogues) for the troublesome Takelma Indians who lived in the region. HBC's John Work, passing through what is now known as the Rogue River Valley in September 1833, referred in his journal to "River Coquin," and the diary text indicates that the name Coquin (Rogue) was already in use by the fur brigades. The river was also alluded to as the Rogue by the Wilkes Expedition in 1841. The Oregon Territorial legislature changed the name to Gold River in January 1854, but by the next year the old name was restored.

About twenty-five miles below Grants Pass, the Rogue River enters a nearly 100-mile-long canyon through the Siskiyou Mountains and makes its final wild, twisting run to the sea. This is the country of the lower Rogue River Canyon.

The lower Rogue River clefts through a realm of impressive geography. Widely known for its beauty and grandeur, the Canyon bisects a wilderness land of lofty mountains, tortuous craggy cliffs, and slopes thick with tall wind-whispering pines and firs, ancient gnarled oaks, and red-barked madrones, where deer and bear far outnumber their scattered human neighbors. In that pinnacled fastness the primal, chilling screams of cougars echo from ravines that see little sun, and eagles patrol the rugged spires and crags above. The Canyon country is, in places, an almost impenetrable region of high mountains, each a backdrop for another, and forested ridges that fall off abruptly into sheer rock walls. Fifteen feet of snow can fall in the higher elevations, and in the spring lush verdant meadows spill from peaks that are often shrouded in sunset-flushed clouds.

Far below this vertical terrain the Rogue River winds between the dark-faced rock cliffs and steep forest walls of the gorge as it dashes down its course to what Lewis and Clark called in their diary "the great Pacific Ocian."

Famous among the world's salmon and steelhead fishermen, as well as people who seek the far, quiet places, the lower Rogue is an impetuous mix of calm and fury. Now gliding through deep, pensive pools, eddying, gentle, the river can suddenly erupt into a roaring, churning cauldron of seething white rapids, with names such as Washboard, Devil's Staircase, and Little Wildcat. Zane Grey, returning many times to the Rogue's siren lure, called it an exciting river and beautiful beyond compare. He found a special place called Solitude Rapids, and wrote a book about it.

Mist-shrouded mountains of the Rogue River Canyon.
(Authors' Photo)

Rogue River Canyon at Devil's Staircase Rapids, circa 1905.
(Siskiyou National Forest Collection)

Approximately thirty miles from the ocean is the mouth of the Rogue's major tributary, the Illinois River. It flows in at the tiny remote community of Agness, a scattering of rustic homes on both sides of the Rogue.

Beyond the western or downstream end of the Canyon the Rogue River widens and flows serenely through gentler topography, the lower, rounder hills of the Coast Range. Still punctuated here and there by riffles, the river forms an island-dotted delta, meeting tidewater about four miles from its mouth. Finally, it enters the Pacific Ocean to mix with the waters of the world.

THE ROGUE, A SPECIAL RIVER

In October 1968, Congress passed the Wild and Scenic Rivers Act, the purpose of which was to save "Unspoiled, free-flowing rivers or river sections that symbolize and perpetuate the vanishing heritage of the original American landscape." The Act recognized that certain rivers in the United States possessed outstanding scenic, recreational, geologic, historic, and cultural values, and it set forth management requirements that would ensure protection of those special qualities.

The Rogue River was one of eight American rivers originally designated a Wild and Scenic River under the 1968 Act. The designated area begins at the mouth of the Applegate River near Grants Pass, and extends for eighty-four miles downstream to the mouth of Lobster Creek. The Rogue includes all three of the classifications set out in the Act: Wild River, Scenic River, and Recreational River.

• • •

The Rogue is a special river, made so not by government edict, but by the lure of its beauty and power and geography, and the people who have lived along its wild shores. It is special because of those who love it. And it is special, in part, because of a unique, nearly century-old human enterprise that is still carried on today, the story of which will unfold in these pages.

CHAPTER 2

Before The Mail Boats

SETTLEMENT ON THE LOWER ROGUE RIVER

Remnants of early Indian culture in the Rogue River Canyon, un-earthed near Marial, five miles upstream from Paradise Bar, have been carbon dated to 9,000 years old. The artifacts are the oldest indications yet found of prehistoric people living along the Rogue. The area of the Marial archeological site was once inhabited by Indians known in historic times as the Takelma. They ranged through the Rogue River Valley and down into part of the Rogue Canyon.

The Indians farther down the Rogue River were of the Athapascan linguistic group. They lived in nearly autonomous family-unit villages of from 25 to 150 people scattered along the river and in isolated creek bottoms. Two of the most influential Athapascan bands on the lower river were the Tututni, who had a number of villages a few miles upriver from the ocean, and the Shasta Costa, who held the country upstream from where the Illinois River joins the Rogue, about thirty miles from the coast.

These early residents found the Rogue River a good place to live. They built sturdy plank and cedar bark huts, sweathouses, and canoes. Game was abundant and the river provided an endless supply of salmon and trout. The fish were commonly caught by an ingenious system of stake-and-pole weirs that channeled them into shallow netting ponds. Mussels were easily gathered, the pearly shells of which were tossed on great mounds. The upriver dwellers also made huge harvests of acorns, which were leached and ground in stone mortars.

The date of the first white presence on the lower Rogue River is not known with certainty. Spanish and English mariners explored the Oregon Coast in the 16th, 17th, and 18th centuries, and it is possible that some of these groups may have seen the mouth of the Rogue from their ships, or might even have landed and discovered the river. Spanish and English coins of the period have been found along the Rogue as far up as Mule Creek, almost sixty miles upriver.

The first positive evidence of white men seeing the lower Rogue River, however, was the documented visit of Alexander McLeod and his party of Hudson's Bay Company men in January 1827. McLeod had been sent to the southern coast of Oregon by John McLoughlin, HBC's chief factor at Fort Vancouver, to gather furs. He was accompanied to the Rogue by a

British botanist, David Douglas, who was exploring and collecting in the Pacific Northwest. It was he for whom the Douglas fir was named.

In 1828 the mouth of the Rogue River was visited again by a white exploring party, when mountain man Jedediah Smith camped there on his way north along the coast from California. And in 1836 the Hudson's Bay Company trading schooner *Cadboro* anchored in the river.

Early traders found the Indians peaceful for the most part, according to existing journal notes and diaries. Some skirmishes did occur, however, as in 1849, when the pilot ship *William G. Hagstaff* attempted to enter the Rogue. The vessel became marooned in low water and Indians swarmed onto it, plundering the stores and burning the ship, while the captain and crew escaped into the mountains. In the summer of 1850, the exploration schooner *Samuel Roberts* crossed the Rogue River bar and lay in the harbor for several days. Hostile natives discouraged a longer stay, but before the *Roberts* moved on several of the crew scrambled atop Elephant Rock, a large monolith in the center of the river, and carved the date and initials of the schooner in the rock face.

Hostilities and skirmishes increased through the early 1850s, both on the lower Rogue and in the inland valley, as more whites, mostly prospectors, began arriving on the Rogue River. Gold seekers from California spilled over into the Rogue River Valley in 1852 when rich strikes were made near Jacksonville, and on the coast gold was discovered in the black beach sands in 1853. Miners worked their way down the Illinois and the lower Rogue Rivers to the ocean, and soon hasty tent towns began springing up like mushrooms north and south of the Rogue. On the south side of the Rogue's entrance, the shantytown of Sebastopol was established. It later became the community of Ellensburg, and still later the name was changed to Gold Beach.

To the Indians, the whites were unwelcome trespassers bent on despoiling and controlling their land. Sporadic raids and ambushes by both sides in the inland valley grew into a major conflict, which was calmed by treaty in 1853. The uneasy truce blossomed darkly into war on October 8, 1855, when a party of whites from Jacksonville attacked and decimated two upper Rogue River camps of Takelma Indians—mostly women and children—at the mouth of Little Butte Creek, north of present Medford.

Revenge by the Takelmas was swift and bloody, and soon the Rogue River Valley and the lower Canyon country erupted into what is now known as the Rogue River Indian War of 1855-56.

On the coast, the Indians remained peaceful, with a few exceptions, for almost five months, though they knew about the battles inland. Then, on February 22, 1856, an uprising occurred near the mouth of the Rogue

Riverside meadow at Big Bend.
(Authors' Photo)

resulting in the deaths of twenty-three whites, including Indian Agent Ben Wright, and the burning of sixty cabins along the river and the coast.

Subsequent battles were fought between soldiers and the natives as the Indian-White conflict raged far up the Rogue River Canyon, with victories and defeats on both sides. The largest battle took place on riverside meadowland at Big Bend, forty miles upriver, where remnants of the soldiers' rock fortifications can still be found in the trees. The last fight on the river was at Painted Rock, downstream from Big Bend. The Indians finally surrendered on June 29, 1856, and were transported 175 miles north to the Coast Reservation, ending a dark chapter in Rogue River history.

• • •

The Rogue River Indian War of 1855-56 signaled an end to native life on the Rogue River. But even before the Tututni and the Shasta Costa and the other bands were driven from their homes, another human culture had begun to establish itself in the ravines and mountains of the lower Rogue country. And in the years following the war, more miners and settlers paddled, poled, and pulled their crude boats and canoes upriver to where the Illinois flows into the Rogue. They went from there by trail farther up into the Rogue River Canyon, where they staked claims and sought level homesites for their families.

Lower Rogue River homestead.
(Rogue River National Forest Collection)

Homestead at Half Moon Bar.
(Siskiyou National Forest Collection)

In the next three decades, the lower Rogue was settled by the type of pioneer who favored the far off, isolated places. It was a hard country to get into and out of, for the only means was by the river itself, or by way of steep, long, winding trails to the "outside."

It is interesting to note that beginning in the late 1860s a number of the Rogue Canyon pioneers were again of Native American stock—Karok Indian women from the Klamath River country in California, who married white miners and came to the Rogue to begin new lives. Such established Rogue River names as Billings, Fry, Huggins, Meservey, and Lowery are examples of this combined heritage.

The settlers and miners who lived in rugged isolation in the Rogue River Canyon country were, like pioneers everywhere, an independent and self-sustaining lot. Living in cabins located on narrow benches, and in scattered riverside meadows, and on the slopes of the Canyon itself, they provisioned themselves from what the land offered. Fish and game were plentiful. The ground was fertile and small gardens and orchards produced potatoes, other vegetables, and such fruits as apples, plums, pears, peaches, and various kinds of domestic berries. Wild blackberries and huckleberries were also abundant. Grassy slopes provided range and pasture for horses. Some river homesteaders had one or two cows, and hogs grew fat on acorns and myrtle nuts. Limited supplies of other necessities were periodically packed in over the mountains by mules.

The pioneers of the lower Rogue River also learned to be expert boatmen. As boys grew to men, much of their time was spent on the water. They came to know every rock, eddy, and riffle, and shooting the rapids of the Rogue became as much a part of their daily lives as fishing and hunting. Sometimes the lessons taught by the Rogue were difficult and occasionally they were tragic. But the ultimate reward of the hard schooling was an expertise in running the river, a valuable and needed skill in a vertical country where the waterway was the road.

THE PROBLEM OF MAIL

One of the major disadvantages of life along the lower Rogue River in the early days was the inability to send or receive mail. It was a frustrating deficiency in what otherwise was viewed by the river residents as an ideal way of life.

The consistent, efficient mail delivery service of today is so much a part of American daily life that it is taken for granted. A short step to the porch or a few paces to a roadside mailbox is usually all the effort required to "get the mail." Packages are brought by parcel post or a private package forwarding company right to the door. But what if such service was not available? What if our letters and cards and business papers and gifts and books and hometown newspapers could not be delivered to us in any timely, organized way? And what if they could not be sent with the same ease? What if there was no mail service available?

Keeping in touch with far distant family and friends through letters is important to everyone, and to those who live in the out of the way places of the world it can be extremely so, a need intensified by isolation. Such desire for communication was sorely felt by the miners and settlers living in remote cabins on the Rogue River in the nineteenth century, for in those days mail was the only means of staying associated in any way with someone outside that vast roadless wilderness.

As the 1890s started ticking down to the new century, there was still no established, organized means of communication whatever into and out of the Rogue River Canyon country. It was not due to a lack of post offices in communities surrounding the Rogue wilderness, for there were a number of early mail facilities outside the Canyon and over the mountains. A post office had been operating in Ellensburg (Gold Beach), at the mouth of the Rogue, since 1863, and one had been established in Roseburg, to the northeast, in the 1850s. Grants Pass, in the valley of the upper Rogue, had its beginnings as a post office and stage station as far back as 1865. The community of Coquille, over the mountains north of the Rogue, was provided a certified post office in 1870.

The problem was that no official postal delivery route served the lower Rogue River from any of those points. Letters trickled into and out of the Canyon through the neighborly graces of whichever prospectors or other river residents happened to be going "outside" on their annual or semiannual trip for provisions. They would take along any outgoing mail as they passed their neighbors' cabins and deposit it in the post office of the town where they were getting supplies. There they would pick up any letters addressed to Canyon residents and deliver them on their return trip.

Often the addresses on the river mail were general, consisting simply of the addressee's name, the creek or section of the Rogue where he or she lived, and the name of a town in that part of Oregon with a post office. Therefore, letters addressed to: "George Watson, Big Bend on Rogue River, Ellensburg, Oregon," were common in those days. That was usually enough identification, for everyone on the Rogue knew where everybody else lived.

Though the unofficial mail carriers were well-intentioned, delivery was uncertain and not reliable. A letter could be written, sent out with a prospector to be posted at Coquille, or Ellensburg, or Roseburg, and chances were that it would reach its destination weeks or months or even a year later. Or maybe it would never get there at all. For it was the nature of the river people to visit each other on their travels, and sometimes to stay as a guest for days or weeks at a time, helping their host with some project or just socializing. There was no hurry in the Rogue country and trail guests were welcome to stay as long as they desired. It was common for trips outside to be delayed along the way—and the mail, too.

If the person going out was a prospector, the letters he carried stood an excellent chance of being completely out of date by the time they were posted. For prospectors often stopped at different places along the river or in the mountains to do some searching for the elusive metal that was the chief focus of their lives. And if they chanced to strike "pay dirt," they would camp right there for a sometimes extended stay.

Three of the Rogue River Canyon prospectors who willingly served as occasional volunteer mail carriers in the 1870s and 1880s were Tommy East, Jim Cloughton, and "Cap" Russell. Stories have been handed down about those three and their good-hearted attempts as "mailmen."

Tommy East was a small, well-known, English-born miner who lived on the Rogue for over forty years. He came into the country during the Indian War and died at age eighty-seven in 1897. Tommy liked to contribute his part by taking out letters on his infrequent trips to town, and bringing mail back for delivery to his friends and neighbors in the Rogue Canyon.

One time Tommy was given a few letters by the Coquille postmaster for delivery to a man named Joe Younker, who had a place four miles up Shasta Costa Creek, a Rogue tributary above present Agness. Tommy took the letters and left Coquille, heading over the mountains to the Rogue. But, in the way of all prospectors, he poked here and there along the route, including lengthy prospecting on Johnson and Rock Creeks. Following that, and doubtless with his mind on hopes of "The Big Strike," the little Englishman went on to engage in serious gold seeking along the Rogue itself, completely forgetting about the mail for Joe Younker.

All that summer the letters remained in the dark recesses of Tommy East's pack. At the approach of winter Tommy shut down for the season and hiked back out to Coquille, where he would stay until spring. As he was unpacking his belongings in Coquille, he came across the undelivered letters. Shamefaced, he took the wayward mail to the Coquille postmaster and asked him to hold it and hope for another way to get it to the Shasta Costa Creek recipient. But with heavy snows in the mountains no travelers passed through.

Spring came and once again Tommy East prepared his pack for the long trail to the Rogue. As he left Coquille he stopped by the post office to pick up any mail for delivery along the river. In the small stack of letters were three worn envelopes addressed to "Joe Younker, Coquille, Oreg., C/O Shasta Costa Creek on Rogue River."

On another occasion, Jim Cloughton, a miner who lived at Old Diggins Rapid, picked up a letter from a neighbor, Alice Isabelle Price, wife of the man who would ultimately bring a boat mail service to the Rogue River. The letter was addressed to Mrs. Price's sister in California. Cloughton courteously told Mrs. Price that he was going downriver and would probably get all the way to the mouth, where he would post the letter. Though nothing was ever said to Mr. Cloughton by Mrs. Price, the letter found its way to the California sister about a year later, after most likely having laid in the Cloughton cabin at Old Diggins Rapid all winter.

Sometimes the well-intentioned prospector-mailmen would carry someone's letter around with them for such a long time that it disintegrated before being delivered. "Cap" Russell once gave a letter to Belle Price which he had carried around in his pocket so long that the envelope had completely worn away. He had then placed the mail in an old sock until he could deliver it to Mrs. Price.

At times a Canyon resident would take letters only part way out, and upon reaching his destination on some creek or gravel bar, would make an effort to pass them on to someone else who was headed in the right direction. It could take weeks, though, to find such a person. On other occasions, mail would be left at a home along the river where travelers would most likely stop for the night on the way in or out, and they would take the letters on.

Such was the state of mail in the Rogue River Canyon country in the early years of settlement. It was sporadic, uncertain, and frustratingly slow.

In the 1890s, with more people coming into the area, the need for mail service on the river became a common topic of conversation. With no roads into the Canyon, and few trails, the only reasonable route left to consider for the transportation of mail was the river.

It was an idea Elijah Price had been proposing for years.

ELIJAH PRICE: FATHER OF THE ROGUE RIVER MAIL BOATS

Elijah Huitt Price was born at Fort Smith, Arkansas on September 27, 1843. He crossed the plains in 1853 with his parents by covered wagon on the Oregon and California Trails to Placer County, California, where his father was a gold miner. Elijah remained in Placer County into his thirties, and in 1879 married pretty Alice Isabelle Powers. Belle had been born in New York state, but at the age of four she and her mother sailed down the Atlantic Coast, across the Gulf of Mexico, and through the Isthmus of Panama, where they traveled by boat and burro. They then went by steamer up the Pacific Coast to San Francisco and on to Placer County, where they joined Belle's father, who had come on ahead.

In 1880 the Prices' first child, Noble, was born at Gold Run in Placer County. The next year, Elijah left his family safe in California and moved north to the Rogue River Canyon, where he worked a gold claim at the mouth of Mule Creek. Two years later, with low production from the mine, Elijah sent for Belle and they relocated their family about fifteen miles downriver to a meadowland farm on a bluff at Big Bend, on the south side of the river. There they farmed and raised a family of seven children.

Elijah Price became a popular leader and spokesman for the river residents, and was instrumental in establishing a school in the district. He also began trying to do something about the mail problem in the Rogue River Canyon. One of Elijah's main supporters in the project was Belle. She had been downright irritated with the lack of mail service on the Rogue even before she moved there, for it had taken from a month to a year to write to her husband at Mule Creek and receive an answer. On May 12, 1883, Elijah Price took the first step in what was to be a long, frustrating, challenging tug of war with the United States government to establish a mail route into the lower Rogue River country. On that day he wrote a letter to Walter Q. Gresham, the postmaster general of the United States. Price proposed that the Post Office Department approve an official, permanent contract mail route up the Rogue River forty miles from the mouth at Ellensburg to Big Bend by boat.

There was an interminable wait for a response to Price's letter to the Post Office Department, due not only to the precise problem he was hoping to correct, but to the creaking, slow-motion machinations of Washington bureaucracy. Finally, an answer: they were not interested. Price pressed on with more correspondence, again pointing out the need for basic mail service. After months of waiting, a terse reply was delivered to E.H. Price, asking the first of what would be a wearisome parade of questions.

The Post Office Department (the name would not be changed to the U.S. Postal Service until 1970) wanted to know about climatic and geographical conditions: How cold did it get in winter? How hot in summer? How wide is the Rogue River? How deep? Then the clincher: How many towns would the route service, and how many families? Price was honest: no towns, about eleven families, a conservative number, for there were many more single miners and settlers in the country. The deal fell through; "Not financially practical," wrote the government.

It had taken Elijah several years to get this far in his proposal for a mail boat service, and he was not about to give up. He wrote again and again, always receiving the same response: "Not practical."

The English philosopher Herbert Spencer said: "Progress is not an accident, but a necessity." He did not mention, though, how long progress could take. After years of rejection by the Post Office Department, Elijah

Elijah Huitt Price.
(Rogue River Mail Boat Trips Collection)

Alice Isabelle Price.
(Rogue River Mail Boat Trips Collection)

Big Bend. Elijah Price's homestead was in the elevated clearing. *(Authors' Photo)*

Price sent his idea of a boat mail to Oregon's famed U.S. Representative Binger Hermann. The congressman, son of a prominent pioneer family, hailed from the Myrtle Point area, north across the mountains from the Rogue Canyon, and Hermann was familiar with the mail problem on the lower river. He was sympathetic to the needs of the Canyon residents and took an interest in Price's boat mail project. Hermann promised to help influence the postal authorities, but warned that even justified changes are slow to be accepted by the government. Elijah Price was already painfully aware of the fact.

Months turned to years as the river settlers and miners waited for some word of progress from Binger Hermann. However, nothing was heard. Rogue boatmen began picking up mail at the Gold Beach post office (the name was changed from Ellensburg in 1890) on their downriver trips for supplies, and in time that office became the chief point for mail addressed to the scattered families up the river. But still the volunteer "mailmen" made only infrequent trips to town.

Meanwhile, the Curry County press was also favoring the proposal for an official mail route up the Rogue River. Articles began appearing regularly in the *Gold Beach Gazette* in the early 1890s promoting the idea. An example was this item from the October 20, 1893 edition: "Residents of the up-river country took advantage of a couple of clear days and came down to the county seat Saturday... As evidence of the necessity of a mail route up the river, we note that they took up a large sack of letters and papers—the accumulation of mail for the Illinois, Big Bend, and Mule Creek country." A large sack of letters and papers was certainly more than the trickle of mail coming into the country a decade before, when Elijah Price first wrote to the Post Office Department. It was now time, more than ever, for a regular mail service up the Rogue. But still no encouraging sign came from Binger Hermann or the Post Office Department.

In mid-January 1894, Rogue boatmen again came downriver, and the *Gazette* announced: "One or two days of good weather early this week brought down a number of the up-river settlers to get mail and see how the rest of the world was getting along."

The Rogue in winter was not to be taken lightly, but good rivermen could always be found to get supplies and mail. They also stood ready for emergencies, as noted in this report in the *Gazette* on January 26, 1894: "The big storm and high river kept most of the up-river people at home, none caring to venture on the dangerous water. There were several, however, that dared it, and did good work, for the sake of a suffering fellow man. When Dr. Tyler was called to Mule Creek, Henry and Wm. Fry met him and took him to the Illinois, and from there Henry Fry and A. Aubery made the trip to Mule Creek and return—all by water. The trip was an extra hazardous and hard one, but willing men were found to brave it all, and in a manner that showed they were fine boatmen."

The next month, February 1894, John and Isaac Fry, Charlie Owen, and A.W. Forgery boated down the Rogue from the mouth of the Illinois. The *Gazette* noted that the men took back with them a "huge sack of mail matter for those living on the upper river. A sight of that mail sack showed the necessity for a mail route up the river."

But still no progress had been made on Elijah Price's proposal to the government. On March 21, 1894 Binger Hermann wrote a discouraging letter to the patient Big Bend settler. The disappointed congressman advised Price that after much study and debate he had been unsuccessful in selling the Post Office Department on the idea of an upriver mail route. The Department officials, wrote Hermann, recognized and appreciated the time and effort expended by Price and Hermann to bring mail service to the Rogue River, but it was simply not economically feasible for the government to provide such a route in a wilderness country peopled only by a scattering of families. It was not practical, the Post Office Department said, and as it was the policy of the Department to determine that new routes were financially sound before approving them, they regretfully had to reject the Rogue River proposal.

Elijah Price, however, was a man of infinite patience and hope. He wrote once again to the postmaster general, by now a Mr. Wilson S. Bissell, and assured him that Price would be happy to prove that the route could be practical and financially sound, if only the Department would suggest how it could be determined.

After another long wait for an answer, Price finally received the first glimmer of hope for his project and an end to the lack of mail on the Rogue. The Post Office Department advised him that the way to prove the feasibility of the proposed route was for Price or someone else to carry the mail up and down the river, one round-trip per week, for one year *at no expense whatever to the Post Office Department.* If, at the end of the year, it appeared that the route was practical and financially sound, and if Price could show them that a mail route up the Rogue River was truly justified, then the Department would establish the route and call for contract bids to operate it on a one-round-trip-per-week basis.

Though the government's suggestion was viewed by Elijah Price and his fellow river residents as a ploy to finally rid itself of the persistent request for a mail route up a wilderness river in Oregon, the stubborn pioneer from Big Bend accepted the challenge. He wrote back to the Post Office Department, agreeing to the no-pay terms of the trial period, and advised the postmaster general that arrangements were underway to implement the route. It was now early in 1895.

Officials at the Post Office Department finally realized the upriver farmer was serious and fully intended to prove the worth of a boat mail on the Rogue. Therefore, they suggested that a post office be established at the upper end of the route so outgoing mail could be canceled properly at that point, then taken downriver. Also, people living in the more remote reaches of the Canyon country would have one central location to pick up their mail after it was brought up by the mail boat from Gold Beach.

The terms of the proposed trial period for the upriver post office were the same as for the new mail route: no pay for one year. And the postmaster to be appointed? Elijah H. Price.

Price happily accepted full responsibility for both the upriver mail route and the new post office. He was appointed postmaster in March 1895, and the little log cabin in which the Price family lived on the ranch at Big Bend became an official, albeit probationary, United States post office. Elijah Price named his new postal station Illahe, after an Indian word *ilahekh*, meaning "beautiful land."

The *Gold Beach Gazette* announced the long awaited upriver mail service on March 15, 1895: "E.H. Price was down from Big Bend during the week... He has just received his appointment as postmaster at Illahe, the new post office that has just been established at the Bend." And in the same issue: "A post office having been established at the Big Bend, and a special route soon to be inaugurated, has awakened the residents along the river."

The next week's edition of the *Gazette* continued the excitement: "...from Washington came the full and complete outfit for the Illahe office. As soon as the latter is delivered and a mail carrier selected, the up-river route will be ready for mail delivery."

The persistence of Elijah Huitt Price had finally made his dream of mail by boat become reality.

CHAPTER 3

Pike Poles And Mail Bags

THE FIRST MAIL BOAT ON THE ROGUE RIVER

Selecting the boatman to act as mail carrier for the trial year was not easy for Elijah Price. The difficulty was not in trying to pick one out of a surplus of willing candidates, it was just the opposite. The prospect of rowing, poling, pushing, and pulling a boat forty backbreaking miles up the Rogue River every week—a trip that would take two and a half days up and one day down—at no pay, did not have applicants standing in line for the job. Some of the rivermen had farms or livestock to tend; many were commercial fishermen, mining the Rogue for its treasure of salmon, and selling their catch to the R.D. Hume Cannery at the mouth of the river. They had families to provide for, and few had time to give away, not even for such a noble cause.

As to who actually took the first mail down to Gold Beach, the record is not entirely clear. Price family tradition has it that Elijah's fifteen-year-old son, Noble, a healthy, strapping lad who was already experienced on the Rogue, was the first mail boatman. But according to the May 17, 1895 edition of the *Gold Beach Gazette*: "Henry Moore came down the river Friday last, bringing the first through Illahe mail. He will make regular weekly trips hereafter, and will carry the mail from his place down. Postmaster Price seeing that it is carried the balance of the way."

Henry Moore lived at the junction of the Illinois River, about thirty miles upriver from the ocean. The Elijah Price ranch at Big Bend was about eight miles further. So although young Noble may well have boated the mail on occasion that spring and summer of 1895, and most likely did help his father with the upper eight miles from the Illinois to Big Bend, it appears from the scant record left to us that Henry P. Moore was the first man to officially take a U.S. Mail boat down the Rogue River to Gold Beach. And he did it on Friday, May 10, 1895.

Old newspaper accounts also indicate that E.H. Price himself boated the mail in that first trial year. Also, another Rogue River pioneer, George Washington Meservey, volunteered as a mail boatman.

The first mail boat was an eighteen-foot, double-ended (both the bow and the stern come to a point) cedar boat built by Moore himself. He had advertised in the newspaper as a builder of Rogue River boats since 1888. The method of propulsion was by muscle, motors not having yet made an

Ladies posing in the first mail boat, 1895.
(Rogue River Mail Boat Trips Collection)

appearance on the river. A sail could be used, too, in the estuary and in the slick-water stretches upriver. Sails took advantage of an interesting Rogue River phenomenon: the wind blows up the river from the mouth to the junction of the Illinois, beyond which it blows downriver.

Rowing was the primary means of moving the first mail boats, and in low water riffles and other shallow places a long pike pole was used to inch the boat along until it could again be rowed. In rock-strewn fast water the boatman had to get out and slowly pull the boat through with a rope attached to the bow, a strenuous technique known as "lining."

It was a hard, tedious job coaxing the little boat the forty miles upriver to Illahe. And it could be dangerous. On one occasion a heavy squall near the mouth of the Rogue hit Henry Moore's sail and capsized the boat. He crawled up onto the bottom of the boat and waved his hat to Chauncy Woodruff, who was on the bank. Woodruff put in a boat and rescued a decidedly damp boatman. The mail sack was saved, too.

The Rogue River mail boat experiment was immediately successful. With the weekly mail runs up and down the river, the previously isolated families upriver to Big Bend finally had regular contact with the outside world. The mail boat only went as far as the Illahe post office, however, which still made it difficult for residents farther up the Rogue River Canyon to send and receive letters. But that, too, would soon be rectified.

Business was brisk for the mail boat in that first year. As early as June 21, less than two months after the initial trip, the *Gold Beach Gazette* was able to report: "The Illahe mail came down on Monday, and on its return Tuesday there was taken up about three times the amount of mail that the sack could accommodate. This is the third time that it has become necessary to have extra sacks to accommodate the mail for that place, and it shows how badly needed the mail service was for that section of the country."

In the months to come, as relatives and friends of people living in the Rogue River Canyon learned that a mail route had been established on the lower Rogue River, a steady stream of letters and small packages went up by mail boat.

In November 1895, a new post office was established at Wedderburn, a small cannery community on the north side of the Rogue River near its mouth. Wedderburn was named after the ancestral Scottish home of Robert Deniston Hume, a salmon-canning magnate who owned the cannery and the company town. Hume also owned the *Gold Beach Gazette* and had its editor, Edwin M. M. Bogardus, appointed postmaster of Wedderburn.

The mail boatmen began picking up the mail at Wedderburn, a decided convenience for the upriver residents, for the new post office was located in the Hume general store, where grocery and other orders could be sent up via the mail boat. Customers along the river could buy a wide variety of goods besides the ordinary supplies necessary for cooking and clothing.

Wedderburn, circa 1898.
(Lex Fromm Collection)

The store inventory listed, among other items: sponges, syrup of figs, Japanese toothache drops, perfume, violin bridges, spectacles, purses, jewelry, books, pencils, pocket knives, toys, bird cages, stationery, guns and ammunition, and a potent powder called "Rough on Rats." The store also supplied boots, butter, coconut, and fresh beef. (The Wedderburn post office is still attached to the general store. The store is now owned by present mail boat pilot Jim Sorber and his wife, Lynne.)

The river-mouth communities of Gold Beach and Wedderburn not only supplied the Rogue Canyon people with mail and goods, they also received certain bounty sent down from upriver farms and orchards. On November 2, 1895, according to the *Gazette*, Elijah Price brought the mail boat down loaded with "...big red apples that were the best ever brought to town." They were quickly gone and of such quality that a number of people placed orders with Price for their winter supply, to be delivered on his next downriver mail trip.

The Rogue River mail boat service was an unqualified success, and was recognized as such by even the cautious officials of the Post Office Department. In fact, they were so impressed with the efficiency and dedication of Elijah Price, Henry Moore, and the other volunteers, that the Department decided early to make the mail run up the Rogue River a permanent contract boat mail route.

So, in the last week of November 1895, less than seven months into the trial year, the Department posted advertisements calling for contract bids to carry the mail between Gold Beach and Illahe, on a one-round-trip-per-week basis all year long. Service by the successful low bidder was to begin on March 2, 1896, and would run for two years, at which time another call for bids would go out.

In November, too, the *Gazette* espoused the general feeling of the area residents that the mail route should be extended upriver from Illahe to Mule Creek by river trail, due to heavy rapids in that stretch, and then over the mountains northeast to the railroad station of West Fork, on Cow Creek, a distance of forty miles from Illahe. On February 2, 1896 the newspaper said that a mail route extending further up the river "would be of considerable benefit to the mining communities in the mountains, as there are a large number of men now there who are entirely cut off from communications with the rest of the world for weeks at a time."

By February all bids for the Gold Beach to Illahe mail route were in, and the low bidder was determined to be, to the surprise of the river people, a man from far away San Francisco, with a bid of $400 per annum. As the March 2 starting date approached, however, nothing was heard from him. When the date had come and gone, and the California entrepreneur had not appeared on the Rogue River, the government awarded the boat mail contract to the next lowest bidder, James Thornton, who lived with his family on the Rogue downstream from the Illinois. The Post Office Department accepted his bid of $600 per year and arranged his contract to run a few months beyond two years to July 1, 1898. The Rogue River had its first paid mail boat operator.

In the spring, summer, and fall seasons of his contract, Jim Thornton used the mail boat for the three-and-a-half-day round trip, but during the high water periods in the stormy winter months he sometimes carried the mail by horseback over a rough circuitous river trail. However, when the river ran as a high torrent of raging water and debris, the trail was likewise difficult to navigate due to numerous windfalls, swollen creeks, and slides. When the mail had to be taken by horse, the whole week was allotted for the round trip.

The river could give a thrashing to boatmen even during normal summer flow, and in winter it could be truly terrible. On one occasion in 1896, Jim Thornton and Ike Fry were making their way upriver in the mail boat in high water, when they came to a place in Copper Canyon, below the Illinois, where a number of dangerous whirlpools had formed. As they tried to pass one, the boat got caught in it and the stern was forced up as the bow went down. Both men were thrown into the brown churning water, and upon surfacing Ike Fry managed to cling precariously to the capsized, tossing boat, while Thornton struck out for shore. He could not get through the rough current and started back for the boat. After almost drowning, according to reports, he was finally able to grab a handhold next to Ike Fry. Together the exhausted men slowly kick-paddled the boat downstream, where they were fortunately rescued by a boat from shore. The nearly tragic incident was an example of the savagery that could be shown by the Rogue in times of high water in the early days.

In the spring of 1896, the Post Office Department, now convinced of the need to provide additional mail service to the Rogue River Canyon, established a post office called Dothan at the West Fork railroad station. James Calvert became the mail carrier on the new route over the mountains from West Fork to Illahe. The trail to West Fork was usually only open as a summer route, however, for heavy winter snows and landslides blocked the narrow trail for months. In fact, Jim Calvert himself was a victim of the harsh mountain winter in 1897, when he froze to death en route to West Fork.

Mail originating from the Portland area and the Willamette Valley, as well as from northern and eastern states, bound for the lower Rogue country, was routed by rail to the Dothan post office and on down to Illahe. Mail coming from the West Coast, including San Francisco, and from states in the southwest, was sent upriver by mail boat. Also brought around to Gold Beach and Wedderburn was mail delayed by winter trail closures at West Fork. In later years all upriver mail would come by boat.

AGNESS, ON THE ROGUE RIVER

In the last years of the nineteenth century, a small cluster of families lived along twin benches of fertile land on both sides of the Rogue at the confluence of the Illinois River. It was a good place to live, with ample level ground for gardens and orchards, and neighbors close by living up and down the Rogue. It was a loose-knit, unhurried, content community of pioneer Rogue Canyon people, with names such as Aubery, Cooley, Fry, Meservey, Moore, and Rumley. The area was a sort of crossroads, or crossrivers, a focal point in the rugged Canyon wilderness.

The district had no real name, it was simply referred to as "Illinois." But in 1897 a name was attached to it that remains to this day, known now by hundreds of thousands of people from all over the world. Anyone who has ever ridden the mail boat knows well the beautiful river community of Agness.

On October 16, 1897 the Post Office Department approved a petition for a post office to be established on the Rogue at the junction of the Illinois. The office at Illahe, on the Elijah Price farm at Big Bend, was eight miles upriver, a long walk for mail. Interest had been shown in having a postal facility at the Illinois two years before during the trial period of the boat mail. Indeed, Elijah Price had requested the placement of a post office there, with Henry Moore as postmaster, and such a facility had been tentatively approved in August 1895. The name of the post office was to be *Cumtux*, an Indian jargon word meaning "to inform," or "to know." But the reality of the office, to be located on Moore's property one mile below the Illinois junction, amounted only to wishful thinking, for the Post Office Department rescinded its approval, stating that a post office at Illahe was sufficient for the trial year of the mail boat.

Therefore, the final approval for such an office in the fall of 1897 was met with cheering support by the people of the district. An area pioneer of 1883, Amaziah Aubery, was appointed postmaster, and he named the new post office at the confluence of the Rogue and Illinois in honor of his daughter, Agnes. Somehow, in transmitting the name to Washington, D.C., an extra "s" became attached, and it was set indelibly in the Post Office Department records as Agness. And it remains that way today.

The mail boat still traveled the eight rapid-choked miles to Illahe, but now the people of Agness received and sent mail from their own post office, a small log cabin soon referred to as the "Federal Building."

Amaziah Aubery held the position of postmaster at Agness until 1901, when John D. Cooley took over. He was replaced in February 1907 by

First Agness post office, 1897. Men are unidentified.
(Larry McLane Collection)

Miller Cooley, and two months later George Washington Rilea was appointed postmaster, remaining so for the next thirty-three years. Mr. Rilea retired in 1940 and died a year later at age seventy-six.

MOTORS ON THE MAIL

The exact date that the first gasoline-powered mail boat started upriver is uncertain, but it is known that Henry Moore was running the first small gasoline launch to haul freight between Gold Beach and Agness in the summer of 1900. The mail boat, with its government regulated schedule, was motorized soon thereafter.

Moore's first boat motor was a one-cylinder, five-horsepower Lockwood-Ash engine, and it is likely that the mail boat motor was of the same type. Vastly underpowered for most of the Rogue, the little gas motors were at least an improvement over rowing in the quieter stretches. But even with the early motors, the mail boat had to be levered over riffles with pike poles, and pulled and pushed around rapids.

The first motor-driven boat to reach Illahe from Agness was operated by Chauncy Fry, also in 1900, but it took him four hours to do it—an average of two miles per hour—with almost constant help from the pike pole. Still, it was an hour faster than could be achieved with a motorless boat. The five main rapids in that eight mile section—Shasta Costa, Two Mile, Old Diggins, Little Wildcat, and Foster—plus the numerous riffles, made for extremely slow going by boat, with or without a motor. Therefore, when the mail boats were motorized at the turn of the century, they often ended their run at Agness and the mail for the Illahe district and points upriver was packed by mule or horse. (In 1908 the mail boats stopped trying to get up to Illahe, except occasionally, and from then on the Rogue River mail route was from Gold Beach to Agness.)

Henry P. Moore, the first mail boatman of 1895, and the man who introduced the Rogue River to the gasoline motor, died in Gold Beach on February 26, 1901 after suffering ill health for some months. His burial was scheduled to take place on his homestead near Agness, and a large number of his upriver friends gathered there to await the ceremony. But such were the moods of the Rogue River in winter, that Henry never made it home. The boat conveying his remains from Gold Beach was so overpowered by high water that the boatman could only reach the Skookumhouse district, about halfway to Agness, and that is where Henry was buried.

The Rogue River mail boat was operated by a number of able men around the turn of the century. The contract to carry the mail changed hands several times between 1900 and 1907, and upon occasion a subcontract arrangement was made when the river mail boatman was prompted by vital farm duties, emergencies, or illness to withdraw. But a carrier was always on the river, or the trail in times of high water, and the mail somehow got through, week after week, year after year, with literally no gaps in service. Some of the 1900-1907 mail boat operators were Nathanial Huntley, Will McLane, Jake and Elihu Fry, William "Billie" French, George W. Meservey, and Ed Huitt.

In those first years of the new century, changes took place in the upriver post offices, too. At Agness, as previously mentioned, John D. Cooley took over as postmaster in 1901 from Amaziah Aubery, who later moved to Grants Pass and began freighting mining equipment to mines in the Grave Creek district. John Day Cooley came to the Rogue River in 1880, where he homesteaded across from the Illinois River junction. He also ran an early inn, the forerunner of one of today's mail boat lunch stops, Lucas Pioneer Ranch.

Around the turn of the century, the Illahe postal facility could have been called the "bouncing post office" for all the moves it made. In 1898 Elijah Price had resigned as postmaster of Illahe and turned full-time to his farm and mining endeavors. He had accomplished what he fought hard to bring about: a workable, organized mail service in the Rogue River Canyon. His replacement as postmaster was James Hall, who held the position for four years, giving it over in 1902 to Ellen Fry, niece of Jacob "Jake" Fry, sometimes mail boat operator and old-time Rogue River pioneer. Jake lived at the Big Bend meadows, on the north side of the river across from Price. Ellen Fry moved the Illahe post office to the Fry ranch, where she presided over mail matters for three years.

In 1905 Ellen wanted to move and give up her job as postmaster. The foreman at the Gold Bar Mining Company, Everett H. Russell, agreed to take the position and was appointed as the new Illahe postmaster. His mining operation was located at Old Diggins Rapid, two miles downriver from Jake Fry's ranch, and the post office was moved down there.

But in three years Elijah Price was again the postmaster, and looked after the Illahe mail until 1918. He left the post office on the north side of the river, crossing over every morning to take care of business, and crossing again to go home at night.

Another post office was approved in 1903 by the Post Office Department for the Rogue River Canyon. This one was twenty miles upriver from Illahe on the side of a mountain at a place called Big Meadows, on the trail to West Fork. It was named "Marial," after the daughter of postmaster Thomas W. Billings. The office soon moved with the family four miles down to the Rogue at the mouth of Mule Creek. Twice-weekly pack trains carried mail between Illahe and Marial, a distance of sixteen miles. (When the Marial post office closed in 1954, it was the last postal facility in the United States to still be served only by mule pack trains.)

THE MAIL GOT THROUGH WITH JOHNNY, FRANK, AND ELIHU

By 1907 motor-powered boats were often seen on the Rogue River, though the horsepower they generated was insufficient for the fast water stretches and pike poles still had to be used. Also, periods of drought in the mountains caused such low water volume in the Rogue that the propellers could not navigate through the many shallow places without striking the rocky bottom.

But motor-powered boats were on the Rogue to stay, and they did allow for faster, more efficient delivery of mail, freight, and groceries. During times of normal water flow a motorized mail boat could travel from Gold Beach to Agness in one day, prompting the Post Office Department to approve a three-times-per-week route for the lower Rogue River. Beginning in that year and continuing for many years, the mail boat left for Agness on Monday, Wednesday, and Friday, and returned from Agness on Tuesday, Thursday, and Saturday.

The new thrice-weekly scheduling allowed upriver residents to receive mail faster and made the mail boatman even more popular, generating

Early gasoline-powered mail boat.
(Siskiyou National Forest Collection)

friendly squibs in a sometimes nitpicky press. In May 1908 the *Gold Beach Globe* referred to Johnny Woodworth, who had the mail contract then, as: "the dependable captain of the upriver boat." He was also called the "admiral of the mail boats"; the "speedy deliverer of Uncle Sam's mails"; and the "commodore of the mail." Johnny and his sputtering little mail boat *Grayling* were much appreciated by the river people, who were glad for the opportunity to send and receive mail with such modern dispatch. They recalled the time, not so long before, when letters meandered slowly, if at all, out of the Rogue River Canyon country in the pockets and packs of prospectors.

Johnny Woodworth's *Grayling* was a twenty-two-foot cedar craft, powered by a ten-horsepower, two-cylinder engine that was known to quit on him smack in the middle of riffles. It could only take the slow ones, it was no good at all in fast water. But the partnership of motor and pike pole most often got Johnny to Agness in time to meet his schedule. He usually left the Wedderburn dock at 6 a.m., and with a normal water flow could make Agness by 5 p.m.—eleven hours of boating, with perhaps a short lunch break along the way.

In the fall of 1908, Johnny's mail schedule was disrupted when *Grayling*'s engine blew up on two occasions. The mail was delayed and the repairs were followed closely in the newspapers with much interest, so valuable was *Grayling*'s service to the people upriver.

Also in 1908 a man named John Franklin "Frank" Lowery began running the mail frequently for Johnny Woodworth. Frank Lowery, who would soon become a mail boat contractor himself, was a likable riverman

Pike-poling on the Rogue River. Frank Lowery, Jr., Johnny Woodworth, Don Lucas.
(Rogue River Mail Boat Trips Collection)

who lived on the north side of the Rogue, halfway between Gold Beach
and Agness. His family welcomed travelers into their large home and the
Lowery place was well-known up and down the river as a center for social
events.

The *Gold Beach Globe* reported in June 1908 one of many such
pleasant occasions at Lowery's, where the guests all arrived by water:
"There was a dance at the home of J.F. Lowery last Saturday night. John
Woodworth, after bringing the mail down, took a crowd from here in his
launch. They report having had a good time."

Another Rogue River boatman who spelled Woodworth on the mail
boat beginning in 1908, and who also would have his own mail contract,
was handsome, twenty-four-year-old Elihu Fry of Illahe. In April of that
year Elihu had been boating heavy loads of hay through the rough water
between Agness and Illahe, a backbreaking job, and according to an item
in the *Globe*, "...(Elihu) does not like the job a little bit." In May, Johnny
Woodworth offered the young, able boatman the opportunity to haul the
mail on the Gold Beach-Agness run. From then on, Elihu Fry was known
up and down the river as a conscientious, efficient mail boatman, unafraid
of high water or storm.

For years Johnny Woodworth, Frank Lowery, and Elihu Fry were the mainstays of the Rogue River mail boat service. Other good boatmen, too, occasionally carried the mail for Woodworth, such as Ed Huitt, Stanley Frye, and Dick Pugh. When the mail boat arrived thirty miles upriver at Agness with one of those three gentlemen aboard, the event usually rated a mention in the press: "Capt. Stanley Frye brought up the mail for Capt. John this week"; or, "Smiling Dick Pugh was the mail boat admiral on Friday." But Woodworth, Lowery, and Elihu Fry were the names most closely associated with the mail boats for the next ten years. Frank Lowery, as will be seen, was linked to the mail boats much longer.

GROCERIES AND PASSENGERS, TOO

In the early years of this century, the first-class letter rate was two cents for the first ounce, and merchandise could be mailed at the fourth-class rate of a penny an ounce, with a package weight limit of four pounds. (Parcel post, with its cheaper rates and more liberal weight restrictions, would not be established by the Post Office Department until 1913.)

The mail boat operators set their own charges for freight, which they carried up along with the mail. The freight cost was usually one-cent to one-and-a-half-cents per pound, much cheaper than the merchandise mail rate. And there were no weight restrictions, except what the boat could carry. Therefore, the upriver residents commonly ordered their groceries and supplies to be sent up on the mail boat as freight rather than mail. Goods that could not be purchased locally in Gold Beach or Wedderburn often did come by mail because the fourth-class rate was still less costly in many cases than a high overland or ocean freight or express charge. Mail order companies such as Sears, Roebuck and Company would cooperate by arranging customers' orders into four-pound packages for shipment by mail.

The mail boats hauled a considerable amount of freight upriver with the mail. The mail boat operators had an advantage over the other river freight boats, especially after the new three-times-per-week schedule came in, because the people in Agness, Illahe, and elsewhere along the river knew that the mail boat would be coming up several times a week with or without freight orders. They could send an order down with the mail boatman and receive the goods soon thereafter. In the summer of 1908, Johnny Woodworth garnered this nice squib from the "Agness Items" column in the *Globe*: "The people of this place find the mail boat a great convenience. Under the able management of Capt. John Woodworth, we get supplies the next day after ordered."

For the delivery of mail to those living in remote cabins along the lower Rogue, the use of individual mail bags came into practice about 1910.

Small canvas bags were sewn by the river residents with their names on them. They were kept at the Wedderburn post office and whenever a letter or other mail came for delivery it was put into the proper bag. On his next run upriver, the mail boatman would toss the bag out onto the recipient's landing. Often the riverside resident would be there in person to receive the mail bag, especially if the boat was also dropping off a shipment of groceries or other supplies. When the person had accumulated several mail bags he or she would give them to the boatman to take back to the post office. Also, letters to be posted were put into the bags and tossed to the mail boatman as he passed by.

• • •

Passengers began hitching rides on the mail boats almost from the beginning. Those who were physically able were expected to help pole the boat over shallow riffles if necessary. All of the early mail boats carried two or three pike poles for use by passengers as well as the boatman. The first passenger fare noted in the records was one dollar for a round-trip, fifty cents one-way, and a charge of from fifteen to forty cents if the person was to be dropped off or picked up between Agness and Gold Beach. Because of mail and freight loads in the small boats, passenger space was usually limited to three or four people, and sometimes there was no room at all.

Low water periods, too, restricted the number of passengers that could be taken upriver. During times of extremely low water flow, one or two passengers and/or a small amount of freight was all that could be boated in one trip. Even then, when the boat came to a riffle everyone had to grab a pike pole or get out and help push and pull the boat over the fast water until the little motor could propel them slowly to the next riffle.

From the earliest days of the mail boats, the Gold Beach newspapers carried running commentaries on who went up or came down on the boats: "M. B. Smith of Agness came down on the mailboat Saturday and will hold down his homestead here for awhile"; "Mrs. G. L. Erluth was the guest of Mrs. J. D. Cooley in Agness this week, arriving on Monday's mail boat"; "E. O. Mulkey, the Solitude Bar miner, walked to Agness this week and came to Wedderburn on the mail boat. He goes to visit relatives at Crescent City." And in 1910, a census year: "Mr. Phil Pearson, the upriver census taker, went to Agness on the mail boat last Wednesday. He is a good fellow, do not hide."

By 1910 there were sixteen gas-motor boats on the Rogue River. A few were for personal use or used for commercial salmon fishing in the estuary. The Hume Cannery owned two, and others carried freight, such as mining equipment, farm seed and supplies, and hay up and down the

Gold Beach, Oregon, circa 1912.
(Larry McLane Collection)

river. Johnny Woodworth had the mail boat, and Frank Lowery and Dick Pugh had their own boats, which were employed, when not carrying the mail for Johnny Woodworth, in freighting jobs.

Three years later, in 1913, the Post Office Department established its popular inexpensive parcel post mail rates. After January 1 of that year, almost anything could be mailed at the rate of five cents for the first pound and one-cent-per-pound thereafter, to a package weight limit of eleven pounds. Soon the weight limit was increased to fifty pounds per parcel for short-haul mailings, and twenty pounds for long distance.

The parcel post system had the potential of a great benefit to the people who lived along the Rogue River, but it would be several years before the postal authorities in Washington approved parcel post to be sent upriver via the mail boats. Most parcel post was shipped by railroad, and the nearest rail point to the Rogue River Canyon was the Southern Pacific line at West Fork, where the Dothan post office was located.

In a decision that left many Agness and Illahe heads shaking, the postal authorities approved payment for a parcel post contract into the lower Rogue River country by mule pack train over the mountains from West Fork to Agness, rather than up the river by gas-powered mail boats. In a related move, the whole lower Rogue River mail contract was changed to include the entire distance from Gold Beach to West Fork, with parcel post coming in by a slow trek over the mountains. The authorities had, however, greatly misjudged the physical difficulties of sending a large amount of parcel post over the rugged mountains and into the Rogue Canyon, due to geography and weather. They also underestimated the volume of packages that the river residents would require to be brought in. The miscalculations soon became evident.

The first contractor to be responsible for the new Gold Beach-to-West Fork mail route was J.J. Weersing of Grants Pass. He was the official administrator of the lengthy route for some years, but being neither boatman nor mule packer, he arranged for others to subcontract the actual work of getting the mail into and out of the lower Rogue.

From 1913 to 1915, Frank Lowery and Johnny Woodworth took turns subcontracting the mail, and sometimes they brought it up together, as indicated in this January 28, 1914 item in the *Port Orford Tribune*, reporting the loss of J. D. Cooley's cow: "...all search seemed to be in vain until Friday when Captains Lowery and Woodworth coming up with the mail discovered her...(and arranged for her safe return to Agness)."

Meanwhile, things were not going well for the mule packers on the West Fork-to-Agness parcel post route, particularly in the winter. Packages of all sizes and shapes were stacking up in the little Dothan post office at West Fork. Mule packers Hank Brown, Dean Walker, Isaac Fry, Charlie Pettinger, and Hathaway Jones were doing the best they could to get heavy loads of parcel posted catalogs, tools, dry goods, and many other kinds of merchandise over the mountains and down into the Rogue River Canyon and on down to Agness.

The distance between Agness and West Fork was about forty miles, much of it almost vertical. The huge amounts of parcel post received in Dothan were often delayed by heavy snow and slides on the perilous trail, so that sometimes Christmas presents sent by parcel post reached the recipient in March or April. An indication of the struggle the packers faced under a mountain of goods in transit can be seen in this short "Agness Item" of December 12, 1913: "(West Fork-Agness) mail carriers do not smile as usual. Just say 'Parcel Post'."

Elihu Fry held the subcontract for the boat mail from January 1915 to March 1918. He was assisted by Frank Lowery, John Woodworth, and Elihu's brother, John Fry. Elihu ran the *Joker*, a trim twenty-two-foot boat with a snug box-like wheelhouse. *Joker* was powered by a twenty-horse-power engine, one of the most powerful motors on the river at that time.

On Saturday, January 6, 1917, Elihu left Agness, coaxing his little *Joker* through turbulent rapids all the way to Foster Bar at Illahe using only the motor, no pike poles or tow rope. The water was running high and Elihu had no extra weight in the boat. The January 11 issue of the *Gold Beach Reporter* suggested that with a little work in the channel, the Rogue could be navigated by gas boats all year from Agness to Illahe, a distance of eight miles. However, though mail boats in ensuing years did run to Illahe on occasion for freight deliveries, passengers, and special mail pickups when the riverside trail was out, the usual mail boat route would always end at Agness.

Mail boat *Joker*, with Elihu Fry in window, circa 1918.
(Rogue River Mail Boat Trips Collection)

Elihu's January 6 trip through the rapids to Illahe had a nice side benefit. According to the *Reporter*, Elijah Price, the man who got everything going back in '95, "...celebrated the event Saturday by sending us down (on the mail boat) a sack of extra large and fine apples, for which he has our thanks. They were fine and we are enjoying them."

Elihu had fun on the way down, too. The *Reporter* announced that: "He made Old Diggins, Two Mile, Shasta Costa, and other smaller riffles under full power enveloped in a sheet of spray and says he had the ride of his life." (It is interesting to note that today's mail boat passengers say the same thing about this stretch of the river.)

CHAPTER 4

Up The River With Bridges, Parcel Post, And A Car

A BRIDGE BY MAIL BOAT

Before 1917 there had been no way to cross the Rogue at Agness except by rowboat, a hazardous experience in spring and winter high water, or by swimming across in the summer, a method only a few were willing to try. It was an inconvenient situation because from its inception Agness was a divided community, half on the east bank and half on the west, and moving from East Agness to West Agness was either difficult, dangerous, impossible, or wet, depending upon the season and means used to cross. It was a settlement split by a river with no bridge. Routine visiting was often out of the question, and going to the post office to mail a letter was bothersome for people in East Agness because the post office was on the west side of the river, as was the school.

In 1916 plans were drawn and funds collected for a high, sturdy, safe suspension foot-bridge to be constructed across the Rogue. Engineering skills for the project came from the U. S. Forest Service in the person of Ranger R.I. Helm. Money to build the bridge was collected from the people of Agness, with some funding by Curry County and some donated by the Macleay Estate Company (formerly the R.D. Hume Company of Wedderburn), which owned a general store in West Agness. The Page Wire Fence Company of Portland was contracted to provide specially made heavy-duty wire fencing for the bottom and sides of the bridge, and planks would be cut to walk on. The span of the main suspension was 365 feet long, and the total length of the bridge from anchor to anchor was 635 feet. It was, according to the Page Company people, the longest bridge of its kind on the West Coast.

Most of the materials for constructing the bridge—cables, bolts, wire, and other supplies—were brought upriver in a succession of trips by the mail boat, under the guiding hands of Elihu Fry, Frank Lowery, and Johnny Woodworth. The little craft was piled high with coils, barrels, and crates of bridge parts. And in the mountains of cargo somewhere were mail sacks—always the mail sacks.

The long awaited bridge, seventy-five feet above the water, with four-foot wire sides that precluded anyone from falling off of it, was completed in February 1917. A grand opening ceremony was held, at-

First bridge at Agness, 1917.
(Scherbarth Collection)

tended by over 150 river residents, and included music, dancing, and a three-act theatrical drama. Among the honored guests at the occasion were "Captains" Elihu Fry, Frank Lowery, and Johnny Woodworth, called by the *Gold Beach Reporter* the "stalwart mail boat crew," who struggled with heavy loads up the Rogue River so that the folks of Agness could have their bridge.

• • •

Meanwhile, the parcel post problem in 1917 was growing worse. Heavy February and March snows had completely blocked the mule trail from West Fork down to Agness and nothing was getting through at that end; no letters, parcel post, or newspapers. Newspapers were particularly important because of the war—the river people wanted to read about it. Even the lower slopes of the Rogue River Canyon were white. Reports to the *Gold Beach Reporter* included one from John Adams, a longtime lower Rogue homesteader, who advised that eighteen inches had fallen at his Potato Illahe Ranch.

Finally, in late March, with snow still falling in the higher elevations, a large amount of the parcel post mail which had been accumulating in the

Dothan post office at West Fork was shipped by rail to Coos Bay, and from there taken down the coast to the mail boat dock at Wedderburn.

Elihu Fry was at the time engaged in necessary work on his Illahe farm, so Frank Lowery arranged to transport the big consignment of parcel post, newspapers, and letter mail up to Agness on the mail boat. The upriver folks were elated, as indicated in the April 5, 1917 edition of the *Gold Beach Reporter*: "The Agness, Illahe, and Marial people who have been waiting a couple of months for papers and parcel post will now be able to catch up on the world's news or the latest style of dress."

Even with the special mail boat run of parcel post, J. J. Weersing reported in late April that four tons—8,000 pounds—of parcel post still remained piled at the Dothan post office. Slowly the mountain of mail receded as Charlie Pettinger, Hathaway Jones, and other packers trudged their mules over the difficult trail and down into the Rogue River Canyon.

The logic and feasibility of having upriver parcel post come by way of the mail boat, even if it was not on a rail line, had been observed by postal authorities. Certain heads in the Post Office Department were beginning to nod affirmatively in the direction of the mail boats. But as is the nature of far away bureaucracies, the wind of change was a slow breeze, and the change in policy that would bring parcel post regularly by mail boat was still four years in the future.

FRANK LOWERY TAKES THE WHEEL

Effective March 1918, the Rogue River boat mail contract was extended to a term of four years. J.J. Weersing was still the prime contractor for the entire Gold Beach-to-West Fork route, but the subcontractor for the Gold Beach-to-Agness section was no longer Elihu Fry, who had quit to pursue other endeavors on the river. In his place came Frank Lowery, who had operated mail boats for Fry and Woodworth for the past decade, and who had been boating freight and people on the Rogue River since before the turn of the century.

John Franklin Lowery was a lifelong Rogue River man. He was born in 1869 at what was then known as Lowery's Clearing, sixteen miles upriver from Gold Beach. He was learning to boat the Rogue's rapids and riffles before he was ten, and as a teenager took people and goods up and down the Rogue when he was not commercial salmon fishing at the mouth of the river.

In 1902 Frank had operated one of the first sputtering gas-motor boats on the Rogue, a small craft named the *Flyer*, in which he carried light freight, and transported passengers to Agness at $3 per round-trip. Lowery had begun running the mail boat for Johnny Woodworth in 1908.

Frank Lowery (in bow) boating mail and freight.
(Rogue River Mail Boat Trips Collection)

Frank Lowery at his dock.
(Rogue River Mail Boat Trips Collection)

Mail Boat *Myra M.* in Copper Canyon, circa 1918.
(Rogue River Mail Boat Trips Collection)

***Myra M.*, in Rogue River estuary, Frank Lowery standing in bow.**
(Rogue River Mail Boat Trips Collection)

When Lowery was awarded the boat mail contract for four years beginning in 1918, he was prepared. His boat, the *Myra M.*, was one of the best on the river at the time. Built by Wesley Miller, the *Myra M.*, named for Miller's daughter, was twenty-six feet long and powered by a four-cylinder, twenty-horsepower engine. She could haul a ton of cargo if there was enough water, for she was a round-bottom boat that needed ample clearance over the gravel bars. The *Myra* had a spacious wheelhouse to accommodate passengers and keep them dry in the renowned Curry County rains.

When Frank had bulky or oversized freight to carry, such as water pipe or lumber, he sometimes used a wide, flat scow built by Johnny Woodworth, called the *War Horse*.

Myra M., left, and Johnny Woodworth's *War Horse*.
(Rogue River Mail Boat Trips Collection)

On March 14, 1918, the *Gold Beach Reporter* announced the change of mail contractor: "J.F. Lowery, known as 'Old Reliable,' is back on the river as mail carrier between Agness and Gold Beach, Elihu Fry, who has been on the job for the past three years having decided he would like a change."

With a reputation for smiling cheerfulness and generosity, Frank Lowery provided excellent mail service on the Rogue, chugging up and down in the *Myra M.* or one of his other boats. He was known as a fearless boatman, so determined to fulfill the responsibilities of the mail that seldom did high water or storms prevent him from heading upriver. Stories about his high water courage and dependability were legion along the Rogue, and he was highly regarded by the isolated upriver people, who saw his mail boat as a lifeline, a connector between their wilderness and civilization.

Along with the mail he carried a wide assortment of interesting freight items—a piano to Agness; a kitchen range to Illahe; a sewing machine to the Will White ranch at Big Bend; a 250-pound cast iron bathtub to the Agness Hotel; and a dismantled sawmill from upriver. Often he carried large volatile loads of kerosene and gasoline, and blasting powder for miners. He also took up livestock—pigs, goats, chickens, and calves. And one year, before Thanksgiving, the popular mail boatman brought down to Gold Beach a number of big Illahe turkeys in what the *Gold Beach Reporter* called "the gobbling mail boat."

There were only three gaps in Frank's tenure on the mail boats from 1918 to 1930. For several months in 1919 he hired George Thornton to run the mail, using Elihu Fry's *Joker*, while Frank attended to family business at home. The Lowerys had taken in travelers since the turn of the century, and in 1919 were building a larger house to accommodate their growing fishing lodge business. "Lowery's on the Rogue" would develop a wide reputation, and a clientele who came far to fish for the famous Rogue River salmon and steelhead.

When Frank again took the wheel of the mail boat after his absence, the *Gold Beach Reporter* announced: " 'Smiling Frank' Lowery has returned to his lost love, and is again navigating the Rogue with Uncle Sam's mail pouches. More power to Frank, he's all the candy."

Other newspaper items in 1919 reported that: "Frank Lowery took advantage of a spring rise in the river to bring record loads of freight to Agness"; and, "A near 'riot' occurred at the Agness post office one day when it was discovered that the week's *Reporters* had not made it onto the mail boat."

And, as always, in 1918 and 1919 the newspapers gave a glimpse of who was coming and going on the mail boats: "Former editor S. E. Marsters came up on the mail boat Monday and will endeavor to place a few attractive life insurance policies during his stay"; "Mrs. Ed Miller went down on Tuesday's mail boat for slight medical attention"; "F. W. Blondell of Agness came down on Tuesday evening's mail boat on business matters"; "Mrs. William Prince came up on Monday's mail boat and is visiting relatives."

There was also this delightful item noted at Christmas 1919: "Frank Lowery, our able and affable mail boat captain, reports taking up to Agness a special passenger on Wednesday's boat, a jolly man in a red suit." The special passenger was en route to a children's Christmas party at the Agness school.

A MAIL BOAT TO THE RESCUE

The spring and summer of 1920 was extremely dry in the mountains of southern Oregon, a consequence of which was the lowest water level ever remembered on the Rogue. The mail boat could not navigate the inches-deep water that flowed over some of the gravel bars, so Frank had to refrain from boating anything other than mail—no freight and few passengers. Even then, using a light boat and hauling only the mail, on several occasions Lowery had to land a mile below Agness. But rains in late August raised the water level in the river. It also brought about Frank Lowery's participation in a lifesaving rescue.

On the morning of August 30, Lowery left Wedderburn with a party of hunters bound for Agness. As he was poling the boat over Wakeman Riffle, upstream from the mouth of Jim Hunt Creek, several of his passengers walked along the gravel bar to lighten the boat. The men noticed a commotion in deeper water ahead. Jack McCadden, a local rancher, had been fording the river with a wagon and two mules, something he had done several times during that low water summer. But the recent rise of the water caught him unaware, and the mules foundered as the current tipped the wagon over. McCadden was thrown into the river and was drowning as Lowery and his party rushed to the scene.

By jockeying the boat, Frank was able to provide a handhold for two of his passengers, who had plunged into the river and were trying to keep the unconscious rancher's head, and their own, above water.

Towing the rescuers and victim, Lowery quickly beached the boat. Then, when the men had laid McCadden on the gravel bar to resuscitate him, the courageous boatman hurried a short distance upstream to where the remaining mule, still connected to the wagon, was thrashing in the water. Running the mail boat onto an exposed bar of gravel, Lowery jumped into the water and managed to free the stricken animal and drag it to shore.

McCadden and the mule survived the ordeal. Lowery gave all praise to his brave passengers for saving a life, and everyone concerned was glad the mail boat had happened by.

• • •

In the fall of 1920, Frank Lowery took his second hiatus from the mail boat service. This time it had to do with the frustrating inefficiency of Uncle Sam's payroll clerks. Frank's contract with the Post Office Department provided that he be paid $1,200 per year, at $100 per month, to deliver and pick up mail at Agness three times a week. The problem was that Frank had not been paid for six months. And that disgruntled him a little. He resigned on September 30 and went to Portland for the winter, joining his wife Annie who was living there while their children were attending schools in the city.

A young man named Firman Wilson took over the job of running the mail boat. Firman was a handsome lad, a favorite with the young ladies of Agness, as indicated in this October 14, 1920 "Agness Item" in the *Gold Beach Reporter*: "The popularity of the new mail carrier is evidenced by the bevy of beauties that assemble at the office to meet the boat when it arrives." The handsome new mail boatman relished the attention and sponsored dances in Agness, all of which were well-attended.

But Firman was no Frank Lowery in Rogue River boatmanship, and he did not care to attempt the navigation of stormy winter high water. The November 25, 1920 edition of the *Reporter* noted: "The river has been a little too high for Capt. Firman, and he is being spelled by Capt. Johnny Woodworth. They don't come too high for him."

Dick Pugh, another old-time river hand, also assisted Firman Wilson on occasion. Overall, however, the upriver residents found the young mail boatman willing, capable, and dependable.

One noteworthy addition to the mail boat service that Firman effected was advertising. The first ever newspaper ad for the "U.S. Mail Boat," showing departure and arrival days and times, appeared in the August 5, 1921 edition of the *Gold Beach Reporter*. According to the ad, a one-way fare to Agness was $2.00, and the price was $3.50 for a round-trip. The ads ran in each weekly edition.

Frank Lowery returned home in August, and in late September began running the mail boat again in place of Firman Wilson. It was an event welcomed by the press, as noted in this September 22, 1921 *Reporter* item: "Capt. J.F. Lowery brought the mail up Monday. It is sure good to see his cheer-

POULTRY RANCH
BEMENT BROS. PROPS.   DENMARK, ORE.

U. S. Mail Boat

LEAVES	LEAVES
Gold Beach	**Agness**
Mondays,	Tuesdays,
Wednesdays,	Thursdays and
and Fridays	Saturdays
at 6:10 A. M.	at 10:00 A. M.

Passenger fare one way, $2.00

Round Trip, $3.50

FIRMAM F. WILSON, Capt.

First mail boat advertisement, 1921.
(Authors' Collection)

Frank Lowery, Jr. and mail boat passengers.
(Rogue River Mail Boat Trips Collection)

ful smile and hear his hearty laugh again.''

Frank must have reached an understanding with his slow-paying Uncle Sam and Firman Wilson. It is certain that he and Firman remained on amicable terms for in October Wilson gave a dance at the Lowery place that the *Reporter* called "one of the most pleasurable events of the season.''

In October one of Frank's sons, Frank, Jr., nineteen, took the mail boat up to Agness for his father. In coming years all three Lowery boys, Frank, Jr. (Frankie), Fred, and Lynman, would become well-known mail boat pilots.

FINALLY...PARCEL POST BY MAIL BOAT

The problem of how to get an increasing flow of parcel post packages to the residents of the Rogue River Canyon continued to plague the mail carriers, local post offices, and the river recipients. The mule pack train mail route had been changed from West Fork-to-Agness to a tortuous river-trail and mountain route from Merlin, near Grants Pass, to Agness. It proved to be worse than the other way in and by February 1921 five months worth of parcel post—much of it Christmas presents—had accumulated at the little railroad settlement of Merlin.

Charlie Pettinger, an experienced packer and himself an Illahe resident, did what he could, but the slow pack trains and winding, difficult route did not allow for anything close to efficient delivery service. Perishables sent by parcel post rotted en route, letters were outdated, and items purchased by mail order, though shipped promptly from the company, were long delayed in arrival.

But at long last, in November 1921, the sage heads at the Post Office Department came to realize the logic of what local Curry County postmasters and Rogue River residents had known all along. On November 24, Postmaster General Will Hays announced that beginning December 1 all mail, including parcel post, bound for Agness, Illahe, and other Rogue River Canyon points, no matter where its origin, would be sent by way of the Rogue River mail boats.

The Merlin-Agness mail route was discontinued, though private freighting kept the mule pack trains on the West Fork-Agness trail for years to come.

The Post Office Department contracted with Frank Lowery to provide the new parcel post service, at a payment of $165 a month for a period of seven months, from December 1, 1921 to June 30, 1922, after which the contracts would run for four years. The contract stipulated that Lowery was to carry up to 400 pounds of parcel post per day, but over that he would be paid an additional $1.50 per hundred pounds to Agness and 50¢ per hundred pounds to Wedderburn from Agness.

Frank was required to make three round-trips to Agness per week under the contract. At first the Department, again showing a marvelous misunderstanding of the conditions on the Rogue River, wanted him to make each round-trip in one day—leave Gold Beach (Wedderburn) at 6 a.m. and arrive in Agness at 2 p.m., then leave there one hour later and arrive back in Gold Beach at 7 in the evening. That schedule, during the winter months, however, would require Frank to navigate the treacherous and high currents of the Rogue during hours of darkness. He could do it, had done so many times, but only for emergency situations, not as a normal routine. It was a foolhardy requirement and before December 1 the official schedule was changed back to the way it had been—one day up, one day back.

Twice-a-week pack mule mail service was established between Agness and Marial, the little post office twenty-four miles beyond Agness, to transport letter mail and parcel post further into the Canyon. Charlie Pettinger had secured the mail contract at that end.

An interesting sidelight to the mail boat story in 1922 was the unique coincidence of three upriver postmasters' names. In that year the postmaster of Agness was George Washington Rilea, the postmaster of Illahe was George Washington Meservey, and the postmaster of the third post office up the line, Marial, was George Washington Billings. The fact of the three "George Washingtons" was noted in *Ripley's Believe It or Not.*

• • •

The new parcel post route up the Rogue River made the river residents happy, but it made "Smiling Frank" Lowery a busy boatman. The inexpensive parcel post rates—five cents for the first pound and a penny for each additional two pounds—brought sacks, boxes, crates, and a myriad of unwrapped items up the Rogue by the ton. Lowery began making extra trips to Agness just to deliver excess parcel post. On January 12, 1922, an "Agness Item" in the *Gold Beach Reporter* announced: "Capt. Lowery brought up two tons of parcel post Sunday (in two boats)." And he did it again the next Sunday, and numerous Sundays after that.

Unfortunately for Frank, however, he lost the route temporarily to Firman Wilson in the summer of 1922, causing the third gap in Lowery's years of mail boat service. When the time came to send in bids for the new four-year contract, to run from July 1, 1922 to June 30, 1926, Frank bid the boat mail job at $1,980, a per-year amount equal to what he had been paid at $165 a month. But Firman bid the route at $1,800 and was awarded the contract.

The *Gold Beach Reporter* ran a long tribute to Frank, and on June 22 noted: "Capt. Frank Lowery will keep his boats on the run, however, to handle the tourist travel which has increased during the past few years owing to the popularity of Agness and Illahe as resort points for sportsmen and recreationists."

The lower Rogue River had indeed become popular with visitors as magazine and newspaper articles began recognizing its scenic appeal. In June 1922, the editor of the *Coos Bay Times* wrote, in an article reprinted by other newspapers: "There is no trip like it in the state... The trip up through the rapids is a novel one and the scenery is simply beautiful. The very fact that Agness can be reached only by making a trip of 32 miles in a small boat adds to the attraction for most people from the cities since they know they are getting back into the wilds."

Frank Lowery's loss of the boat mail route was temporary, though, for in November of that year Firman Wilson, having personal problems, left the mail boats and "Old Reliable," as the newspapers called Frank, took over the contract. He remained the mail boat operator until 1930.

ANOTHER BRIDGE BY MAIL BOAT

In February 1923, Siskiyou National Forest Supervisor E. H. McDaniels and an engineer came up to Agness on the mail boat to arrange for the

This 1924 Agness bridge was brought upriver by mail boat.
(Scherbarth Collection)

construction of a 380-foot suspension bridge over the Rogue River, suitable for horses, mules, and light wagons.

By summer all the plans had been made, workers hired, and tons of bridge construction material shipped in to the Wedderburn docks. In the fall, when rising water flow on the Rogue allowed the transport of heavy loads, and with newspaper reports closely following the progress of the project, Frank Lowery began hauling tools, equipment, sacks of cement, iron bolts and fixtures, and coils of cable upriver in his mail boat, the *Myra M.* Also crammed onto the little boat on every trip were pounds of letter mail, mountains of parcel post, and passengers. Laboring continuously under heavy loads, the *Myra*'s motor burned up and Frank replaced it with a new, more powerful Ford engine.

Each landing of the mail boat at Agness was greeted by an enthusiastic group of local supporters, anxious and elated to have the newer, larger bridge underway, and thankful to Frank and his sons for their tireless efforts. Now the Agness folks would not only be able to cross the river, but do it on horseback or in a light wagon (there were no automobiles in Agness yet). The nearby 1917 foot bridge was also scheduled for strengthening and renovation.

For the transportation upriver of the heavy main suspension cables and such oversized items as large wooden and steel beams, Frank was assisted by John Woodworth, Dick Pugh, and Ran Meservey in Woodworth's scow, the *War Horse*.

Eventually, the piers were set, the anchors put in, the towers built, and the crossway and deck constructed. The entire project took nearly a year, with delays caused by winter high water and inclement weather. The bridge was opened for pedestrians, horses, pack trains, and one-way travel for narrow wagons on June 24, 1924. A festive celebration was held to officially open the bridge and to honor those who made it possible, including Frank "Old Reliable" Lowery. It was the second bridge Frank and the mail boat had helped bring to Agness.

MORE PASSENGERS, THE SHERIFF, AND THE BLACK COW

Through the decade of the 1920s, Frank Lowery had great success and continuing acclaim as an excellent mail boatman. He was always on the go, running extra trips every week, sometimes at night, to keep up with the deluge of parcel post. There were still no roads into the Rogue River Canyon country, and parcel post continued to be the best means the upriver people had to bring in goods. Anything that could be fit within the liberal weight and size limits (fifty to seventy pounds, depending on the zone of origin, and no more than eighty-five inches in combined length and girth) was mailed in by parcel post.

Nails, shovels, picks, dry goods, heavy mining machinery parts, and most groceries came by parcel post. So did sacks of cement, window glass, hardware of all kinds, plumbing supplies, and coils of chicken wire and fence wire. Tons of gold ore from upriver was shipped out as parcel post. Farm seed and animal feed also came in by parcel post. In a two year period, Frank Lowery took more than fifty-five tons of barley by mail boat to upriver points, all mailed as parcel post.

Holiday mail made him even busier. On December 2, 1923, Lowery carried 3,300 pounds of parcel post to Agness, the largest load of cargo ever brought up in a single boat. And in the ten days between December 10 and December 20, 1923, Frank carried more than six tons of parcel post and regular mail to the people living along the Rogue.

During these busy mail boating years, Frank often stayed in a small Macleay Estate Company cottage at the mouth of Indian Creek, on the south bank of the Rogue across from Wedderburn. The Gold Beach postmaster, J. D. Fay, had the mail delivered to the Indian Creek dock, then Lowery chugged across to Wedderburn, picked up the mail there that had come in from the north, and started upriver with his load.

Mail matter headed upriver from Agness was in the charge of Charles H. Pettinger, who had thirty mules and employed several packers to handle the job. Charlie or one of his men, "Dutes" Blondell, Will Collins,

Agness Hotel (now Lucas Pioneer Ranch), circa 1916.
(Bernard & Clarice Jackson Collection)

Pettinger's lodge at Big Bend Ranch.
(Bob & Monica Doerr Collection)

Hathaway Jones, Burl Rutledge, Will Thornton, Carl Wood, or one of the others, would line up a string of pack mules in front of the Agness store and post office and pack up mule loads of parcel post and freight to be taken along the Rogue River trail to Illahe, Marial, and cabins in between.

Frank had a new and larger boat built to better accommodate his increasing loads of mail and passengers. He called the new mail boat the *Limit*, and often it was filled to that. In years gone by he carried one, two, or even three passengers on a trip, but in the mid-1920s he was frequently taking from five to eight people at a time, local folks and visitors.

On upriver and downriver trips the mail boat stopped at Lowery's Lodge for lunch. At Agness, sightseers and fishermen were well-accommodated at Sadie Lucas Pettinger's Agness Hotel, built in 1916. Sadie and Charlie Pettinger also welcomed guests on their riverside Big Bend Ranch at Illahe, land once owned by Jake Fry. The spacious ranch house, originally named Hunter's Lodge by its 1919 builders, Will and Susie White, was home to hundreds of solitude-seeking vacationers over the years from such far away cities as New York, Los Angeles, San Francisco, and Portland. (The lodge burned in 1959.)

• • •

Occasionally, the long arm of the law reached into the Rogue River Canyon, and it arrived on the mail boat. Curry County Sheriff Floyd "Peck" Huntley, or his Gold Beach deputy, Cleve LeClair, from time to time made excursions up the Rogue with Lowery to investigate a theft or a death. And once in awhile one of the passengers on the downriver trip wore manacles and a sad expression.

Peck was sheriff from 1920 to 1928, and during those Prohibition years Rogue River Canyon moonshine sold in Gold Beach for up to $20 a quart. So, periodically he also took the mail boat up to arrest whomever was making Gold Beach "high spirited."

Other lawmen, too, rode with the mail on runs upriver, including state officers, postal inspectors, and at least once, a U.S. marshal.

• • •

Not all Frank Lowery's passengers were of the human variety. As mentioned earlier, the mail boats carried ones that clucked, oinked, gobbled, and bleated, too. In March 1923, with Johnny Woodworth's help, Frank took up on the mail boat sixteen nervous sheep for Charlie Pettinger. And in the fall of 1924, he transported as parcel post thirty-five rabbits, bound for Postmaster George Washington Rilea at Agness.

Then there was the black cow.

The story is told that in the summer of 1925 or so, an Agness homesteading family named Edgerton wanted a milk cow. Norman Edgerton learned a cow that gave good milk was for sale in Gold Beach and he purchased her sight unseen.

Now he had his cow but needed to get her up to his home at Agness. He knew that Frank Lowery freighted just about anything on the mail boat, so why not a cow? He enquired of Frank, and yes, Lowery would bring the animal up on the boat.

So on a morning soon after, a truck rolled down to the mail boat dock at Indian Creek, across from Wedderburn, with a cow. A very big, black, nervous cow. But something the seller neglected to tell either Norman Edgerton or Frank Lowery was that this particular cow hated men. After unloading the cow from the truck, there followed a long ordeal of trying to get her aboard the mail boat. The cow, never having been on a boat before, had no intention of going on this one, and not liking to have men handle her anyway, began kicking, lunging, and bellowing at Lowery and his helpers.

At one point the fellows had her in the boat and were in the process of snubbing her ropes so that she would be safe, when she gave a mighty kick and fell out of the boat into the water, thrashing in the shallows. Though the men got the unruly cow quickly up on dry land, they had an even more difficult time trying to get her back onto the mail boat.

Finally, she was aboard and heading upriver. Frank Lowery had thought that she would calm down once the boat began droning its way up the estuary, but the cow continued to kick, bellow, and strain at the ropes. Going through the riffles was even worse, particularly Crooked Riffle, with its curving stretch of rough water.

Eventually, after the eight-hour boat ride, Frank and his helpers and one mad black cow made it to the Agness landing. Then came the problem of getting her out of the mail boat, a procedure fully as difficult, amidst kicks and lunges, as was getting her aboard downriver. She was finally coaxed, pulled, and pushed out of the boat onto the gravel bar landing and led up the hill to the Edgerton place. She still disliked men, and now she disliked boats. But Norman Edgerton had his cow.

Another mail boat adventure involving the Edgerton family occurred some time after the cow episode. Fred Lowery, one of Frank's sons who often took a turn piloting the mail boat, was about to pull out of Agness on the downriver run one morning, when suddenly a messenger brought the news that Clarissa Edgerton, Norman's mother, was in dire need of medicine from Gold Beach.

Fred made the down trip in record time, got the medicine from Dr. James Wheeler, and immediately started back upriver, reaching Agness after dark. The grateful Edgertons received the medicine from their hero mail boat pilot, then Fred headed downstream again in the Rogue River night to get the boat back to Gold Beach for the next day's upriver run. It was the first time ever that the mail boat had made three consecutive trips, down, back, and down again, much of the time in the dark.

• • •

Frank Lowery was awarded the 1926-1930 boat mail contract on a bid of $2,295 per year. This time, though, he was required to haul, in addition to letter mail, up to 600 pounds of parcel post on each trip, an increase of 200 pounds over the previous contract. The mail runs were still three times a week; up on Monday, Wednesday, and Friday, back down on Tuesday, Thursday, and Saturday. The excess parcel post went up on Sunday.

• • •

On September 15, 1928, Frank Lowery boated a car to Agness. Edward Miller, automobile editor for the *Portland Oregonian,* had learned that genial Agness postmaster George Washington Rilea had never been in an auto. There were none in Agness—no roads to get there—and George had seldom been "outside." Miller, sensing a great publicity stunt, arranged with Frank Lowery to take a Chevrolet roadster upriver on a boat. Frank had managed to boat a small Ford up to his ranch earlier that year, but never had anyone attempted to take an auto on a boat up through the fast water and narrow canyons to Agness.

With the approval of the Chevrolet Motor Company, a Portland

Frank " Old Reliable" Lowery, *Sunday Oregonian,* September 30, 1928. *(Authors' Collection)*

dealer volunteered the use of a new car for the project. Ed Miller and a friend set out for Gold Beach in the gleaming roadster, and on Sunday, September 15, at 7:30 a.m., met Frank Lowery and his sons Fred and Frankie (Frank, Jr.) at the Bagnell Ferry slip, four miles upriver from Wedderburn.

The front bumper and top were taken off and the Chevy was carefully run up on planks and into the open boat. The rear of the car rested up on the edges of the bow and the back wheels were taken off. Frank then ran the boat out into shallow water and rocked it back and forth. He said the load was top-heavy, but he thought he could probably make it to Agness. Then, with Ed Miller and several others following in a boat piloted by Frankie, and with comments from the nervous Miller about the new car falling into the Rogue River, Frank Lowery, accompanied by son Fred, headed for Agness.

In the quiet stretches the auto-weighted boat sped along at eight or so miles an hour. But in the riffles Frank had to go slow, jockeying the little boat into narrow channels, and sometimes scraping the gravelly bottom, the propeller spewing stones and water like a machine gun.

They pulled into Lowery Lodge for a rest and lunch, then headed upriver again. Through Coal Riffle and Sherman Riffle they went, then plowed through Nail Keg, Bear, and Boiler Riffles. To get past a couple of the riffles, the second boat was used to tow the car boat. At Crooked Riffle, where strong currents made sharp right-angled turns, Frank had his hands full guiding and coaxing the boat into the fast water, skillfully avoiding tipping the car over into the river. When he was through, he grinned his famous grin, and waved his hat at the other boat.

At Smith Riffle, just below Agness, Frank and Fred were forced to pole the boat through the shallow water, the propeller again grinding gravel.

At 5 p.m. they reached Agness, and after spending one and a half hours unloading the Chevrolet, the first automobile in the Rogue River Canyon chugged up to the Agness post office. The next morning, Mr. George Washington Rilea had his first ride in a car.

That afternoon the auto was again carefully loaded onto the boat and Frank took off for Gold Beach. He had little difficulty on the downriver trip, but above Crooked Riffle he tied the boat to a tree and pondered the situation for thirty minutes. Then he went through, and, according to Ed Miller: "When he finally took it, the boat turned its sharp corner as if in still water. Mr. Lowery, we affirm, is a superb boatman." A long, illustrated article in the Automobile Section of the *Sunday Oregonian* on September 30, 1928, described the adventure.

Boating a car to Agness, *Sunday Oregonian*, **September 30, 1928.**
(Authors' Collection)

Unloading the Chevrolet at Agness, *Sunday Oregonian*, **September 30, 1928.**
(Authors' Collection)

Agness Postmaster George Washington Rilea, *Sunday Oregonian*, September 30, 1928.
(Authors' Collection)

The empty shell of "Lowery's on the Rogue" still stands as a riverside landmark.
(Authors' Photo)

Frank Lowery stopped running mail boats in 1930, when he was sixty-one, but he remained a Rogue River boatman for many years. His fishing resort, Lowery's on the Rogue, became a well-known headquarters for tourists and fishermen from all over the world, including Bing Crosby, who visited numerous times. The lodge closed in 1959, and Frank Lowery passed away in 1963 at ninety-three years of age. The empty shell of the venerable old lodge still stands and is pointed out to passengers by today's mail boat pilots in memory of Frank "Old Reliable" Lowery, the premier mail boatman of the early days.

CHAPTER 5

Big Cargos And Hollywood Stars

The decade of the '30s brought changes and new names to the Rogue River mail boat service. The 1930-1934 boat mail contract was awarded to Roy E. Carter and his partner, Oscar E. Miller. Neither were boatmen themselves; Carter was manager of the Gold Beach Motor Company, the local Ford dealership, and Oscar Miller was also associated with the firm.

Though not rivermen, they were able businessmen and saw the opportunity to operate the mail boat service as a profitable business, providing good service with top employees and new, modern equipment. In that they succeeded and for twelve years, from 1930 to 1942, the names Carter and Miller were synonomous with the Rogue River mail boats.

A great improvement in the Rogue River mail service began with an amended agreement to the 1930 contract. The contract had been awarded to Carter and Miller on their bid of $2,950 for a three-trip-per-week route to begin on July 1. But three months later, by mutual consent, the schedule was increased to six round trips a week to Agness, up and back on the same day. Daily mail service had come to the Rogue River Canyon. Under the terms of the new schedule, effective September 28, 1930, a Carter-Miller boat would leave Gold Beach every day, except Sunday, at 7 a.m. and arrive at Agness by noon. It would then leave Agness at 2 p.m. and arrive back at Gold Beach by 5 p.m. The daily schedule ran from May 1 to October 31. From November 1 to April 30, the boats were on the old three-day-a-week run; up on Monday, Wednesday, Friday, back down on Tuesday, Thursday, Saturday, due to less daylight and high water in winter.

Under the new contract, Carter and Miller were also required to carry up to 2,500 pounds of parcel post on each daily and thrice-weekly trip. The pay was $4,320 per year, plus $1.50 for each 100 pounds of parcel post over 2,500.

The Carter-Miller mail boat fleet consisted at first of three brand-new twenty-six-foot, round-bottom, double-ender cedar boats built by Johnny Woodworth. They were open boats, designed for ten passengers. The engines, sixty-horsepower, four-cylinder, Model A Ford motors, were positioned amidships. The passengers and/or cargo sat in front of the engine, and the boatman stood at the rear of the engine behind a raised spoked steering wheel.

The new mail boats had an ingenious arrangement for raising the propeller as high as sixteen or eighteen inches whenever the boat was about

Tom Fry piloting a Carter-Miller mail boat, circa 1930.
(Authors' Collection)

Propeller and rudder lift assembly, used for shallow water. Fromm-built boat.
(Authors' Photo)

**Carter-Miller mail boat pilot Earl Johnston, circa 1931.
Note propeller-lift chain at bottom of photo.
Stepping on the chain raised the propeller and rudder in shallow water.**
(Rogue River Mail Boat Trips Collection)

Mail boatman Abe Fry, circa 1930.
(Abe Fry Collection)

to enter shallow water, so that it would not drag in the gravel. The idea was developed by commercial Rogue River fishermen Dick Fisk and Charlie Graber in the late '20s. The propeller shaft, running through the boat from engine to stern, was coupled to a universal joint that allowed the end of the shaft to be raised yet continue to rotate the propeller.

It worked by a system of pulleys and chain hooked to a hinged bar assembly off the stern of the boat that was itself attached to the propeller shaft running horizontally out of the boat near the bottom. (See photo.) The chain was stretched low across the inside of the boat where the pilot stood at the wheel. He rested a foot on the chain when approaching a low water riffle, then gunned the engine hard into the shallow water and at the same time he stepped down on the chain. When the chain was depressed, it raised the whole propeller and rudder assembly off the gravel bottom until the boat reached deeper water again. The propeller-lift was used on the mail boats for over twenty years.

To pilot the new mail boats, Carter and Miller hired the best men available, including Earl "Skipper" Johnston, a commercial fisherman and expert Rogue River boatman; Dick Pugh, an experienced and popular mail boatman from the Woodworth and Lowery days; and Ran (Randolph) Meservey, a longtime Rogue boatman. In 1930 Carter and Miller also hired as a mail boat pilot young Abe Fry, nephew of Elihu Fry (operator of the 1915 mail boat *Joker*), and great-grandson of upriver pioneer Jake Fry of Big Bend. Abe had been working as a mechanic at Roy Carter's Ford agency, and was already, at twenty-two, a skilled Rogue boatman. Carter and Miller offered him the opportunity to work full-time at his first love, boating the Rogue River, and he gladly accepted, staying with them as one of their finest boatmen for twelve years. Two of Abe's brothers, Tom and Norman, and a cousin, Claude Fry, also boated the mail and freight for Carter-Miller.

Three years later, in 1933, Carter and Miller would hire an eighteen-year-old lad named DeForest Sorber to make upriver runs for them. They were not concerned about entrusting their boats and freight consignments to the youngster, for he had been running the river as a licensed boat pilot since he was fourteen (after fudging his age on the Coast Guard forms). Prior to being hired by Carter and Miller, he had been taking his own boat loaded with freight all the way to Paradise Bar, over fifty miles upriver, for the mining operation of Count George Hay DuBarry, a concert pianist turned gold miner. (DeForest Sorber would later have his own boat mail contract in a well-known longtime partnership with Lex Fromm.)

Abe Fry going through Crooked Riffle.
(Rogue River Mail Boat Trips Collection)

Mail boatman Tom Fry with Roy Carter.
(Authors' Collection)

RIDING THE "ROGUE RIVER EXPRESS" IN 1930

For a glimpse of what it was like to ride the mail boat over sixty years ago, here are excerpts from a delightful account by Lawrence Barber of his trip to Agness in September 1930 (published in the *Sunday Oregonian*, January 1, 1931):

"The woods people of the lower Rogue have their only connection with the outside world by means of shallow-draft boats which daily carry the mail and supplies from Gold Beach to Agness and Illahe, thence inland by pack train ... taking food and news, joys and sorrows to the people of the mountains.

"On this particular September morn, we arrived at the appointed boat landing four miles east of Gold Beach before anyone else was there ... There were three small craft there, each about 26 feet long, drawing about one foot of water and powered with nothing more or less than a model A Ford motor. And when the boatmen arrived we found that not one but two would be needed to carry the day's freight and express, mail and passengers to Agness.

"There were seven passengers on hand that day ... Mr. Carter assigned four to one boat and three to the other. Boxes of freight and express, bearing labels of mail-order houses and department stores in Portland, San Francisco, Chicago, and New York, and packages from other businesses in Gold Beach, Marshfield, and Crescent City, were heaped in the bow of the boats, and mail pouches were tossed into the stern beside the engineer. Passengers were assigned seats midway.

"The pilots adjusted their gas and spark levers and pressed buttons to start their motors. Both motors roared, as unmuffled Fords will, and the propellers churned water as we pulled away from the landing.

"Our pilot evidently knew his course well, for he picked his way upstream, sometimes hugging one bank, sometimes the other, and often midway of the two shores. As we approached riffles he swung the boat squarely into the fastest current to give his craft the advantage of the greatest depth of water. It was in bucking these riffles that we experienced the greatest thrills of the journey. From the downstream side we could often barely see the quiet water above the riffles, so high were they. Two, three, four feet the boat would climb against the current, chugging and churning in the shallow water, the propeller picking up stones and gravel and tossing them behind like a Fourth of July pinwheel.

DeForest Sorber taking it through Crooked Riffle, circa 1934.
(Rogue River Mail Boat Trips Collection)

The "Rogue River Express" in Crooked Riffle.
(Bob & Monica Doerr Collection)

"Moving upstream at an average rate of eight miles an hour, we noted the increasing height of the surrounding hills, becoming more and more heavily timbered as we advanced toward the interior.

"And now and then the boatman, as official mail carrier of the lower Rogue, stopped the motor and slid the nose of the craft onto the sand long enough to drop off mail pouches and packages. At times the sandy bank itself was the only mail box to be seen. Settlers and summer residents came down to the river to meet us and exchange greetings. They picked their day-old copies of *The Oregonian* out from their mail to learn the latest news from the 'outside.'

"At Lowery's ranch we left a larger supply of freight and express, supplies, we presumed, for the Lowery homestead, a boarding place for sportsmen. Here lives J.F. Lowery and his stalwart sons... and scattered up and down the river we saw their guests casting for steelhead and trout...

"We were landed at a gravel bar a short distance below the junction of the Illinois and Rogue Rivers. At the landing stood the shell of a small motor truck which the pilot referred to as the 'mail truck.'

"Agness, we found, consists of three buildings—a store, a hotel, and a private residence—all many hundred yards apart in a clearing high above the river.

"The mail, freight, and express were loaded into the truck and the mailman took his place as driver, chugging away to the store and post office, three-fourths of a mile away.

"Agness is a sort of community center, for here all the folk from the hidden valleys and hunting lodges in surrounding hills gather for mail and supplies and gossip. Trappers, traders, prospectors, hunters, and anglers make this their mail address, unless they go to Illahe, eight miles above, or Marial, 17 miles farther.

"At Agness, Postmaster Rilea sorts the incoming mail and redistributes some of it to mail pouches for the upriver communities. Charles Pettinger, who holds the mail contract above Agness, employs four youths to carry for him. They ride with strings of pack horses from Agness to Illahe and on to Marial, the post office of the Mule Creek mining camp.

"The mail boat runs on from Agness to Illahe when passengers make it worth while, but the climb is great and the trip treacherous because of the climb of 295 feet in a distance of eight miles, as compared to a climb of 105 feet from Gold Beach to Agness.

"The upstream trip required 3½ hours, but the return voyage to Gold Beach was made in less than 2½ hours. Running with the current, the mail boat zoomed over the fastest riffles at top speed. Now and then we narrowly missed colliding with boulders jutting up in the rapids. From time to time the mail carrier slowed up enough to pick up mail pouches hung out for us on poles stuck up in the sand or from racks.

"The express calls at all gravel bars and inhabited flats, wherever it may serve the people of the lower Rogue with its cargo of mail and supplies and joys and sorrows."

The round-trip fare to Agness and back on a Carter-Miller mail boat in 1930 was a modest $3.00. But then Roy Carter's Ford agency was selling brand-new roadsters for $435, and deluxe Town Sedans for $670.

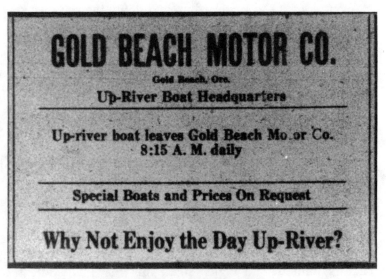

Carter-Miller mail boat ad, 1930s.
(Authors' Collection)

ANOTHER BRIDGE GOES BY MAIL BOAT

The transporting of freight, in addition to letter mail, parcel post, and passengers, was an important part of the Carter-Miller Rogue River mail boat operation. Boats bigger than the twenty-six-footers were needed to take up large cargos of freight, so the partners had a number of twenty-nine-, thirty-three-, and later, thirty-six-foot boats built by Fred Sorber, a boat-building craftsman and father of DeForest Sorber.

Even routine freight shipments could be dangerous on the Rogue. On a late fall afternoon in 1931, Abe Fry was coming down the river from the Ponting-Marsh Mill with a boatload of heavy beams the size of railroad ties. They had been loaded crossways in the boat and piled so high that Abe could not see the bow of his boat. As he entered a choppy riffle, the boat suddenly took on water and sank. Abe dove into the swirling river and managed to swim to shore, narrowly avoiding being crushed by the askew cargo of beams. The load and boat were later recovered.

The first really large freight contract for Carter-Miller was awarded in the late summer of 1931. A new steel suspension bridge was to be constructed by the U.S. Forest Service across the Rogue at Agness to replace the existing one. The previous horse and light wagon bridge had been so damaged in a 1927 flood that it was safe only for light pedestrian travel.

The new steel bridge would be 663 feet long and eight feet wide, ample for the one-way crossing of motor vehicles. The actual construction would be handled by the Clackamas Construction Company of Oregon City, and by September tons of bridge-building equipment and material ordered by the company was piled and stacked at the Carter-Miller landing near Gold Beach.

Agness suspension bridge,
transported upriver in 1932 piece by piece in Carter-Miller mail boats.
(Bob & Monica Doerr Collection)

The boats had to wait for a rise in the river to accommodate the heavy loads. In early October came a slight deepening of the water flow and the boatmen began a feverish pace of hauling 3,000-pound loads of steel girders, hardware, cables, lumber, machinery, and 40-tons of cement, up through the Rogue River riffles to Agness. In addition, of course, the mail boats carried the usual boatloads of parcel post, and during that summer and fall of 1931 they carried 1,200 passengers up and down the river.

The new bridge was completed on April 21, 1932, the first motor vehicle span in the Rogue River Canyon, and again the mail boat company had a large participation.

CCC DAYS ON THE MAIL BOATS

The largest cargos ever brought up the Rogue River were taken by the mail boat company as part of Franklin D. Roosevelt's "New Deal" program.

The Civilian Conservation Corps, the flagship program in President Roosevelt's depression-era relief effort, put young men to useful work on projects in the nation's forests, such as planting trees, building roads and trails, and fire fighting under the supervision of the U.S. Forest Service.

The CCC came to Curry County in the spring of 1933, with several massive camps planned for the Siskiyou National Forest. One such camp was to be established at Agness, where the projects would include: building a road between Agness and Illahe; the construction of two fire lookout houses; the start of a long-term road building project from Illahe over the mountains to Powers; and miles of forest trail maintenance.

Roy Carter and Oscar Miller won the contract to haul the men, equipment, food, and supplies for the 200-man camp to Agness on their boats in the summer of 1933. They also contracted to bring up numerous pieces of heavy equipment, the likes of which had never been carried on Rogue River boats. Several of the machines posed new challenges to the mail boat company. Like the 16,000 pound tractor...

In an article under the heading "Heavy Tractor Goes To Agness," the *Curry County Reporter* on June 22, 1933, described in some detail the historic conveyance to Agness of a giant Cletrac tractor with attached grader, having a combined weight of eight tons. The monster machine was let down the ramp at the old Bagnell Ferry landing, about four miles upriver from Wedderburn, and onto a small motorized scow. The weighted scow settled deep in the water, showing leaks here and there. Two Carter-Miller boats were hooked in tandem to the scow by long ropes. Abe Fry and his cousin Claude piloted the boats, with Abe's brother Norman as skipper of the scow.

This tractor-grader combination, weighing nearly eight tons, was the first heavy equipment to be boated upriver.
(Siskiyou National Forest Collection)

Progress was slow up the river, and the low-sided scow was taking on water in the riffles. Within a few miles, the temporary tow post buckled and everything had to be halted midstream while repairs were made. Then it was on to Lowery's Lodge for lunch and a rest, where it was decided that a third boat was needed, as well as boards to build up the sides of the scow before any further riffles were attempted. Soon another mail boat, piloted by Earl Johnston, was attached to the "river train," as the newspapers called the procession, and again the big tractor was underway to Agness.

Better progress was made with the help of Johnston's boat, and though the engines were laboring, no further mishaps occurred until Crooked Riffle. Darkness was settling down on the river as the three boats and scow entered the churning waters of Crooked Riffle, with its hard right angle turn, and the boat motors were working at full speed. Suddenly, the scow began swinging wildly in the current twisting the tow ropes into a confused tangle. Lines were made fast to a shore rock and a tree so that the tow ropes could be straightened out as quickly as possible. Meanwhile, the heavy scow was swinging crazily between the eddy and the current, and was dipping into the water, taking a goodly amount into the craft as the scow crew bailed furiously.

By the time they were ready to go again it was pitch-dark. The boats struggled through Crooked Riffle and on toward Agness, the experienced pilots guiding themselves by points on the canyon rim and dim outlines of riverside landmarks.

Finally, the shore lights of the waiting CCC crew came into view. The boatmen of the mail boat company had brought their cargo safely through, as always. They were treated to a midnight supper at the Lucas Hotel, then sleep. The next morning they returned to Gold Beach. They had cargo to deliver.

• • •

The mail boat company would bring up two more tractors—six tons each—that summer of '33, as well as a five-ton compressor, trucks, and other machinery. DeForest Sorber, who was one of the primary boat pilots on the massive CCC freight movements, recalls taking up gasoline in big drums weighing about 500 pounds each. He could take four drums at a time on the boat he was using—a ton of gasoline on a little open river boat pushing up through the fast water of the Rogue River to Agness.

Later, Sorber ran what Carter-Miller called the "CCC boat," a special daily mail boat that took up letters, groceries, and small freight items to the boys in the woods. It also carried men upriver to the camp, mostly city fellows who had never before been exposed to such beauty as they saw along the Rogue River. The fir-clad ruggedness of the Canyon and the free, tumbling spirit of the river left imprints on many of them, and changed some forever.

In the spring of 1935, the big CCC camp, officially known as "Agness Camp F-45," was being changed over from a tent city to one with a full complement of permanent wooden buildings. DeForest Sorber, Earl Johnston, Frank Lowery and his sons, the Fry boys, and other boatmen, such as Ruel Hawkins and George Thornton, were kept busy by the mail boat company hauling loads of lumber—280,000 feet of boards, posts, and beams—on river boats and on a special forty-five-foot scow built for the purpose. The scow was pulled by three boats and took seven hours to make the journey to Agness. They also carried hundreds of feet of water pipe, and plumbing fittings in 500-pound barrels. More heavy equipment went up, too, including three bulldozers, three graders, six trucks, and several lighter vehicles. It seemed a long time from that day in 1928, just seven years earlier, when Frank Lowery boated up a Chevrolet roadster so that George Washington Rilea could have his first ride in a car.

Meanwhile, the regular Carter-Miller mail boats were carrying over a thousand passengers and tons of parcel post a year on their daily trips to Agness. In addition, upon the completion of the CCC road between Agness and Illahe, an eight-mile truck delivery of mail and parcel post to the Illahe post office was made a requirement in the mail contract.

In the fall of 1937, Agness Camp F-45 was closed and all of the equipment not remaining for use by the Forest Service was boated back downriver to Gold Beach. The CCC contracts had brought a hectic four years to the Carter-Miller enterprise, with extraordinary challenges to boatmen and boats. But, as always, the mail boat company delivered.

THE MAIL ORDER LODGE, AND "STUART X"

Through the 1930s, a significant amount of mail boat business came from owners of summer homes, some quite palatial, located along the river in the area of Agness and Illahe. Such a number of these seasonal residents were well-to-do, that the newspapers and local people began referring to that section of the Rogue as "Millionaires Row." Though the term was an exaggeration in some cases, the fact was that many of the new arrivals were successful business people from other states. They could well afford a high measure of luxury in their homes, and many freighted in fine woods, tiles, and furnishings. Everything was brought up by mail boat or independent boatmen, such as Ran Meservey and Ruel Hawkins.

California businessman A.T. Jergins was the first of the "new" Rogue River settlers, buying Elijah Price's old ranch at Illahe in 1926. Then came wealthy Los Angeles industrialist W.S. McFarland, Roscoe Oakes of San Francisco, attorney A.L. Dorn from San Diego, W.P. Swope of Hollywood, and Chicago physician D.L. Powell, among others.

Most of the newcomers ordered the building supplies for their riverside homes to be brought up as regular freight. One cost-conscious new arrival, however, a true millionaire oil man and executive officer of the Fox Film Corporation, had almost an entire, full-size lodge sent upriver—by mail.

His name was Stanley Anderson, and he first came to the Rogue in 1929. He bought property at Cherry Flat, between Agness and Illahe, and in 1930 purchased the old Billings ranch in Marial at the mouth of Mule Creek, twenty-four miles upriver from Agness. He chose the Marial property for his home and immediately made plans to completely renovate the large turn-of-the-century farmhouse that was there, almost from the ground up. He also planned to build a spacious guest house and other buildings.

For a reason known only to Mr. Anderson, perhaps simply as an eccentric cost-saving scheme, he arranged for every piece of building material to be sent upriver by parcel post mail. A postmaster's report at Gold Beach noted that Anderson was having such items as: "cement and plaster...fancy bricks, tile, lath, and other building materials" mailed by parcel post "in ton lots and even greater quantities." He also ordered a half-mile of water pipe, which was cut and threaded in six-foot lengths so it could come by parcel post. He sent for roofing material, kegs of nails, boxes of hardware, cans of paint—all to come by mail for his great building project. After coming down the Coast Highway in trucks, the supplies were put aboard the mail boat and taken up to Agness, where they were loaded on mules and packed upriver to Marial.

The mail boats had often been asked to transport unusual cargo, but that was the first time they carried as Uncle Sam's mail an almost complete Rogue River lodge.

• • •

Another eccentric fellow who sought the tranquility of the Rogue River Canyon was a wealthy investor and world traveler from Berkeley, California named Henry Clifford Stuart. By his mysterious choice, however, Henry was known on the river only by the strange appellation, "Stuart X."

In the summer of 1930, Stuart X purchased several adjoining properties on the north bank of the Rogue at Illahe, whereon he built a beautiful home which he called Minnewakon Lodge. Residing at the lodge were Mr. X, his wife, a maid, and a male servant, as well as occasional guests from around the world.

Stuart X's connection to the mail boats was this. Before coming to the Rogue River, he had never bought anything from a mail-order house. But after discovering the delightful catalogs of Montgomery Ward, Sears, Roebuck and Company, and others, offering a vast array of merchandise that could be ordered in the comfort of a remote Rogue River home, he became an overzealous mail-order customer. He began sending for anything that temporarily struck his fancy, whether he needed it or not, and it all came by parcel post. Boxes, crates, rolls, and some items without containers started showing up on the mail boats for Mr. Stuart X, Illahe, Oregon. He obtained more catalogs from companies all over the country, and he began buying through the mail from companies that did not even have catalogs.

Furniture, kitchenware, rugs, clothing, tools, jewelry—anything that could come up the river as parcel post, he bought.

The problem was that Mr. Stuart X was a particular man and not easily pleased. So, most of the things he bought through the mail were promptly returned the same way. A 1935 report by Postal Inspector R.C. Shelton noted that Stuart X purchased no stamps at the local Illahe post office, but once a month was sent a large supply from San Francisco. He also had his own postal scales and parcel post zone information. It was certainly all

Carter and Miller mail boat dock at Ferry Hole.
(Rogue River Mail Boat Trips Collection)

legal, and only came to the attention of the postal authorities through an inspection of the Illahe post office.

For years the kindly but eccentric gentleman received a continuous flow of parcel post packages, and an almost equal number of parcels left Minnewakon Lodge to be returned to cities "outside." And though the Rogue River mail boatmen may not have recognized the name Henry Clifford Stuart, they knew only too well the more familiar "Stuart X."

CELEBRITIES RIDE WITH THE MAIL

By the 1930s, the Rogue's scenic wonders, relaxed pace, good fishing, and convenient proximity to California, made it a favored haven for people constantly in the public eye. Many heard about the Rogue from colleagues, and some read about the river paradise in magazine articles and books by such noted authors as Zane Grey, who first saw the river in 1919 and later built a cabin at Winkle Bar near Marial. Grey's 1928 book *Tales of Fresh Water Fishing* primarily describes his steelhead fishing and camping trips on the Rogue. His 1929 novel *Rogue River Feud* was also sited along the river and includes a favorite camping place of the author, Solitude Bar, upriver from Illahe, where he wrote much of the book.

Zane Grey lived and wrote on the Rogue River.
(Authors' Collection)

Distinguished visitors to the Rogue over the years were numerous, seeking rest and recreation and momentary refuge from the demands of their careers. They stayed at the Sunset Inn in Gold Beach, or one of the several rustic lodges near the mouth of the river. And many of them looked forward to the scenic adventure of a mail boat ride up the famous Rogue River to Agness.

Celebrity visitors in the 1930s and 1940s, included: John Barrymore, Joan Blondell, Myrna Loy, Dorothy Kenyon, Wallace Beery, Jackie Cooper, and Tyrone Power. The British actor Nigel Bruce rode up with the mail, as did playwright Leland Hayward. Freeman Gosden and Charles Correll—"Amos 'n Andy"—went up on Carter and Miller's mail boat, and Van Heflin, Will Geer, and Jeff Chandler made the trip as well.

Famed author William Faulkner saw the river from the mail boat, and so did J.P. Marquand (creator of the Mr. Moto series), who later bought property in Gold Beach and along the river. Ernie Pyle enjoyed riding with the mail, and wrote his last book at the Sunset Inn. The award-winning MGM cinematographer Irving Rees, who filmed such screen classics as *The Good Earth* and *San Francisco*, fell in love with the lower Rogue and took the mail boat trip a number of times.

Carter-Miller era mail boatman Abe Fry, now retired on a farm near Powers, told the authors about the time he took "Fibber McGee and Molly" upriver on a pleasant summer day in 1939. "They were nice, polite folks," Abe said of Jim and Marian Jordan, the real-life married couple whose radio program was popular across the nation from 1935 to 1957. The Rogue River was far away from Fibber McGee's jam-packed closet ("Don't open that closet, McGee!") at "79 Wistful Vista Lane," and the

Jordans relished the break from their hectic schedule. Abe remembers that Jim Jordan waded up to his belt in cold Rogue River water on that trip, helping Fry get the boat over a troublesome shallow riffle.

Bing Crosby and his bandleader brother, Bob, both born in the Pacific Northwest, were veteran riders of the mail boats, and occasionally spent time fishing at Lowery Lodge.

Of the famous personalities who visited the Rogue in the 1930s and 1940s, however, none is more closely associated with the river and the mail boats, and indeed Oregon itself, than a man named Clark Gable.

Born William Clark Gable in 1901 at Cadiz, Ohio, Billy Gable, as he was known, spent two years in Oregon during his struggling days as a young actor. He arrived on a freight train at Bend, Oregon in 1922, where he worked in the woods and in a sawmill, while saving his money. He next went to Portland, looking for work in a local theater company. He sold neckties at the Meier & Frank store to make ends meet, then joined a traveling theater troupe in Astoria under the name William Gable. The Astoria Stock Company played Columbia River towns in Oregon and Washington and closed in Portland. Billy Gable next worked on a surveying crew on the Oregon Coast, picked hops in the Willamette Valley, and worked in a lumberyard in Silverton, east of Salem. Then it was back to Portland, where he joined another theater group, while selling ads for *The Oregonian*, installing telephones, and working in a garage. Finally, it was off to California and his future as Clark Gable, the King of Hollywood.

Clark Gable,
frequent mail boat passenger and Rogue River fisherman.
(Authors' Collection)

Clark Gable was a consummate outdoorsman, and fishing and hunting occupied a great deal of his leisure time. On his first trip to the Rogue in 1930 he was captivated, returning almost yearly for fishing and rest over a period of time that spanned nearly three decades. He liked to stay at the Sunset Inn in Gold Beach, and often arranged to be guided for salmon and steelhead by Gordon Asher, a well-known Rogue fisherman. Sometimes Gable would fly over to Grants Pass and visit his friend Rainbow Gibson at his We-ask-u Inn lodge, also on the Rogue, and fish at that end.

Clark Gable loved taking the mail boat trip, and Abe Fry recalls piloting the star up to Agness with the mail on a number of occasions. According to Fry, Gable was easy to talk to and a knowledgeable fisherman. Once in awhile Clark would ask to be put off on a remote gravel bar to fish and be alone for a time with his own thoughts, then be picked up on the mail boat's return trip downriver.

In 1934, Gable came to the Rogue after finishing an exhausting schedule in the filming of a picture called *Manhattan Melodrama*, which introduced Mickey Rooney and co-starred William Powell and Myrna Loy, herself a Rogue River visitor. On that trip, happy to again be in the element he preferred, the star garnered a delightful little squib in the local paper: "Mr. Gable rode with Abe Fry in the mail boat Wednesday. The actor proved an able hand when he jumped out to help push the craft over a shallow bar of gravel upriver."

In later years Emmett Kelly, King of the Clowns, and George "Gabby" Hayes would also ride the Rogue in the mail boat. And in the 1950s, Football Hall of Fame great Norm Van Brocklin, former University of Oregon player and star quarterback of the Los Angeles Rams, was so taken with the lower Rogue, which he visited often, that he requested that upon his death his ashes be scattered on the river. (His wish was carried out in 1983.)

And then there is Bobby Doerr.

THE BALLPLAYER AND THE SCHOOLTEACHER

He first saw the Rogue River from a mail boat in the fall of 1936. He was eighteen years old, a young Pacific Coast League ballplayer from Los Angeles, in Oregon for an off-season vacation at the invitation of Les Cook, his trainer, who had a cabin at Illahe. He was so captivated by what he saw on that boat trip up the Rogue that he stayed until spring, purchasing property overlooking the river at Illahe. That mail boat had taken him into a country he has called home for fifty-five years.

The young ballplayer from California was Bobby Doerr, whose meteoric rise as a record-setting second baseman for the Boston Red Sox would one day lead him to the Hall of Fame.

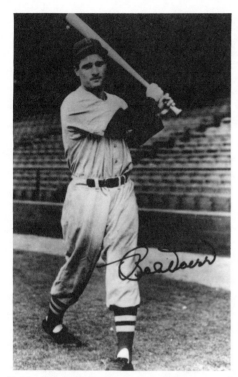

Bobby Doerr, Hall of Fame second baseman for the Boston Red Sox, 1937-1951.
(Bob & Monica Doerr Collection)

Bob and Monica Doerr, Illahe, 1938.
(Bob & Monica Doerr Collection)

Besides discovering the Rogue River that year, the winter of '36 was significant for Bob Doerr in two other ways as well. First, he met the pretty schoolteacher who had come to Illahe the year before to teach in the tiny one-room schoolhouse. They were introduced at a Saturday night dance at the Civilian Conservation Corps camp in Agness. Her name was Monica Terpin and she lived with Mr. and Mrs. Charles Pettinger at their Big Bend Ranch. Charlie had charge of the mail route between Illahe and Marial at that time, and Monica still remembers the strings of pack mules at the ranch and the colorful packers who boarded there.

The young schoolteacher was attracted to the polite, soft-spoken baseball player from California, and when he was not off exploring in the woods or fishing and she was not teaching, they found lots to talk about on river outings and picnics.

Also, before the spring of '37, the talented minor leaguer was signed to play for the great Boston Red Sox and was in the opening lineup at Fenway Park that year. It was the beginning of a fourteen-season career with the club.

At the end of that first major league season, Bob returned to the Rogue and was welcomed by the friends he had made, including the young schoolteacher. They were married in the fall of 1938 at the close of his second year with Boston.

The mail boats figured prominently in the lives of Bob and Monica Doerr in those early years, as they did in the lives of most Rogue River Canyon residents. The boats took the couple out each spring for the start of the baseball season, and brought them back in the fall. They received their groceries by mail, as well as sacks of fan mail for the popular Red Sox star. Baseballs and even bats were brought upriver by the mail boats for Doerr to sign. (Indeed, he still receives all of his fan letters by mail boat.)

The mail boats were true lifelines for Bobby Doerr on two occasions of medical emergency. In 1938, shortly after Bob and Monica were married, he was chopping a tree on a hillside. It fell as it should have, but started to roll. Dodging away, Bob inadvertently ran into his axe causing a serious gash in his leg. He was in a terrible fix; the Rogue River Canyon was not a convenient place to have a bad injury, especially one that had the potential of ending a budding career in major league baseball, for the nearest doctor was in Gold Beach.

Fortunately, the accident occurred on a mail boat day and the boat was still at Agness. With Monica's help, Bob managed to make it to the new Agness-Illahe road put in by the CCC boys. It was the practice of the mail boatman at that time to haul the mail by small truck the eight miles to the Illahe post office. Bob and Monica were picked up in the mail truck and taken to Agness, where the injured man was loaded aboard the mail boat.

Neither Bob nor Monica now recall who the mail boat pilot was that day—perhaps Earl Johnston or Abe Fry or one of the Lowery boys. But one thing is certain: that boatman broke records getting down the river to Gold Beach.

When they arrived, Bob's leg was treated by Dr. W.A. Cartwright, the lower Rogue River's only physician from 1929 until 1947. Dr. Cartwright had seen many injured people come down on the mail boats, and often he went upriver on the boats himself to see patients. On one occasion the doctor was going up in a private boat, when he met the mail boat coming downriver fast with an injured person aboard. The boatmen brought the boats close together in the middle of the river and the doctor nimbly climbed over into the mail boat to treat the wounded man. Dr. Cartwright was seventy-nine years old at the time.

Under Cartwright's skilled hands, Bob Doerr's injury responded well and soon he and Monica took the mail boat home.

Two years later, in December 1940, Bob was again helped by the mail boat in a medical emergency, when he was sped down to Gold Beach with a ruptured appendix.

But most of the mail boat trips were pleasurable for the Doerrs, and a few were exciting. Like the time they were trying to get home to Illahe in 1941 after a trip "outside" to visit relatives for Christmas.

The river was high, brown, and turbulent, with lots of drift, branches and logs, coming down. "Monica was pregnant with our son, Don," Bob told the authors, "and it was a big, high river, but we had to get home. We got on Earl Johnston's mail boat with two or three other people, confident that he could run the river.

"But when we got up to Copper Canyon the water was just boiling through there. It's a narrow place and it didn't look too good. Earl said he would take us over to the south bank and have us hike up over the mountain and meet him on the other side after he took the boat through alone. It would have been a heck of a walk, and with Monica pregnant and all, we decided to go on through with Earl.

"There was a pretty fair load in the boat, with the others and us and all the luggage. At the time I had never run the river myself (Bob later became a river guide and respected whitewater boatman), but I was always fascinated by the guys who could run it when it was like that. So Earl said he'd try it and off we went.

"The river was fast and rough in there and it kept holding the boat back. Then a big slick boil would form and he'd run up through that. Then the boat was held back some more until another boil would form, and he'd go through that one. And that's how Earl got us through Copper Canyon on that trip. It was a rough go, but we made it all right."

Bob and Monica still live on the Rogue, and in a sense, Bob Doerr still has a connection to the mail boats, though he is usually unaware of it. Because each time the present mail boat pilots on the 80-mile and 104-mile whitewater trips bring their boatloads of passengers back down through Illahe, they say something like this: "And now, for all you baseball fans, if you'll look up on that hillside on the right, you'll see a green roof in the trees. That's the river home of ... "

BOB ELLIOTT TAKES THE MAIL IN '42

The Carter-Miller mail boat years came to an end in early 1942, when the Post Office Department accepted Robert C. Elliott's bid of $3,600, which was $300 lower than that submitted by Roy Carter, for the 1942-46 contract term.

Bob Elliott, from Marysville, California, had maintained a summer place on the Rogue near Gold Beach for some years before moving to

Bob Elliott and his mail boat, circa 1942.
(Authors' Collection)

Oregon in 1942. After acquiring the contract he did not advertise much and did not go after the big freighting jobs as did Carter and Miller. Bob had only a few boats, but passengers were scarce for the war was on and tourism was at an all time low. That did not discourage Bob Elliott; he carried local people and visitors when they came, delivered the mail, and enjoyed being on the Rogue River.

Bob became a fairly adequate boatman, though much of the time, he hired more experienced rivermen—Ruel Hawkins or Frank Thornton or one of the Lowerys—to run the mail upriver.

On September 15, 1943, the Illahe post office was permanently closed, and the mail boat carrier became responsible for delivery of Illahe mail directly to roadside boxes on the eight mile stretch between Agness and Illahe. For this he used a truck that was kept at the Agness boat landing.

Bob Elliott's tenure with the mail boats was short, only the length of one contract term. When the 1946-50 boat mail contract was opened for bids on December 11, 1945, Elliott submitted an amount of $5,200. The contract was awarded to lower bidders, who proposed that they would carry the mail for $4,600 per year.

Their names were Lex Fromm, DeForest Sorber, and Kenneth Meservey.

CHAPTER 6

Riding The Riffles With Fromm And Sorber

When three friends, Lex Fromm, DeForest Sorber, and Kenneth Meservey, bid for and won the 1946-50 Gold Beach-to-Agness mail contract, it signaled a new era for the Rogue River mail boats. It was the beginning of growth and change that would gradually bring nationwide fame to the little boats named for places on the river they plied, such as: *Skookum House, Copper Canyon, Crooked Riffle,* and *Miss Agness.*

The mainstay of the new enterprise was a farseeing innovator who, with the help of an experienced, dedicated partner, nurtured and guided the business to the point where a trip up the Rogue River by mail boat became one of the most popular recreational attractions on the Oregon Coast, enjoyed by thousands of visitors each year. His name was Lex Fromm.

Lex was born in Curry County and got his start as a Rogue boatman in 1919, when, at the age of ten, he guided fishermen who were staying at his Uncle Will White's lodge at Big Bend. Lex lived for some years on the Sixes River, as well, where his parents had a dairy farm. After high school, Lex attended Southern Oregon College of Education, and graduated with a teaching degree. He taught for twelve years in Gold Beach, and when not in the classroom he was on the river. He built his first river boat in 1935, and even certain class projects had to do with boats or fishing, as when he helped his students make and sell bamboo fishing rods to raise money for the support of the school track team.

Fromm was principal of the school in 1943 when he was called into service in the Navy. Upon his discharge in 1946, Lex returned home to the Rogue with a desire to earn a living on the river. It was then he learned that the Post Office Department was opening bids for the boat mail contract.

• • •

DeForest Sorber, more commonly known on the river as "Fat" Sorber (a nickname given to him as a youth), was born at Gold Beach in 1915. When he was twelve, DeForest worked on gillnetting boats, and by fourteen, as noted earlier, he was boating freight upriver for Count George Hay DuBarry. He joined Carter-Miller in 1933 and for several years drove mail boats and freight boats to Agness and the CCC camp. DeForest also hunted for gold and worked in the woods, but his heart was always on the river. When bids came open for the 1946-50 boat mail contract, DeForest talked to his friends, Lex Fromm and Kenneth Meservey.

Kenneth Meservey, member of a pioneer Rogue River family and grandson of Illahe postmaster George Washington Meservey, was the third partner in the contract for a short time, but after a couple of months he left the business. Fromm and Sorber would remain partners for thirteen years.

The first order of business for the new mail boat operators was to get some boats. They could have obtained Elliott's fleet, but those were round-bottom boats, sluggish and inefficient in times of low water. Lex and DeForest wanted a design more compatible with the vagaries of the Rogue River water levels. So, after Sorber and Meservey found a shed of good cedar lumber in Grants Pass, the partners had Fred Sorber, DeForest's father, build two new boats for them with a more efficient, nearly flat semi-V hull design. Each was equipped with propeller-lifts, and when Chevrolet truck engines were installed the boys were ready to go.

Passenger business was slow during that first season of 1946, though Lex and DeForest were kept hopping with big loads of freight and parcel post—sometimes two or three tons a day. The contract called for six round trips per week from May 1 to October 31, and three trips per week during the winter. From Agness, they ran the mail up to Illahe mail boxes by truck, but sometimes slides and washouts made a trip through rough rapids to Illahe necessary. "There was a little road between Agness and Illahe," Lex Fromm recalled. "But it was not very good, and sometimes in the winter you couldn't get up to Illahe. We'd have to run the boat clear up in that high water and some Illahe people would meet us at the river and deliver the mail for us. It was kind of mutually agreed upon by all concerned to cooperate and see that the mail got through in those days."

In 1947 the mail boat passenger business started picking up. The post-war economy was strong, there was a building-boom going on, and increasing numbers of people were again spending leisure time in recreation and travel. More Oregon Coast visitors began taking a ride on the mail boats for relaxation and to savor the scenic beauty and wilderness of the Rogue River Canyon.

Passengers also enjoyed the novel experience of "riding with the mail," and seeing letters, parcel post, and freight delivered to isolated homes, lodges, and camps along the river. Lex Fromm recalls there were as many as twenty individual mail stops on the river in the 1940s. Occasionally, passengers would be treated to the sight of dogs running down to meet the mail boat and fetching the mail sacks up to their masters.

First Fromm and Sorber boat at mouth of the Illinois River, 1946.
(Rogue River Mail Boat Trips Collection)

**The first Fromm and Sorber mail boat dock was located
at the base of the Rogue River Bridge in 1946-48.**
(Rogue River Mail Boat Trips Collection)

Lex Fromm driving *Skookum House*, pulling into Agness, 1948.
(Rogue River Mail Boat Trips Collection)

The *Crooked Riffle* coming up through Crooked Riffle, 1948.
(Rogue River Mail Boat Trips Collection)

DeForest Sorber hauling the mail above the E. E. Combs place, circa 1947.
(Rogue River Mail Boat Trips Collection)

To keep pace with the growth of the Rogue Boat Service, as Lex and DeForest called their mail boat business, in 1947 and '48 they began building additional boats, working far into the night after coming off the river. There was almost always one or more boats in various stages of construction in the boat shop, for Lex was also building boats for other people to supplement the income from the new business. In the winter, when water conditions allowed, the partners also contracted to tow log rafts from above Lowery's Lodge to downriver sites.

BILL LANE LENDS A HAND

Although the passenger excursion part of Rogue Boat Service was steadily growing, by the end of the 1948 season Fromm and Sorber were still only taking fifteen to twenty people a day up to Agness and back—3,000 or less for the six-month spring, summer, and fall season. It was far more productive than earlier years when the Carter-Miller boats carried seven or eight passengers, and Bob Elliott fewer than that.

Lex and DeForest, however, knew that there were many more potential customers out there; vacationers and sightseers, who would enjoy the exhilarating, unique experience of the upriver boat trip. For these folks to

An early Fromm and Sorber mail boat.
(Lex Fromm Collection)

line up at the mail boat dock, though, they would first have to find out about it.

Fortunately, both Lex and DeForest were nice fellows, courteous and generous (they still are). So when a gentleman and his wife and two daughters from California approached them on a day in 1948 and asked if they could take a short boat ride out into the estuary for some fishing, the mail boat captains said sure, why not. Lex was not doing much at the moment, and he enjoyed showing travelers the Rogue he loved. He put the family aboard a little boat and took them out around the bay, then up the river for a ride and some fishing.

Lex and the visitors got on well together from the beginning and the man was grateful for the courtesy shown by the young mail boatman. The man from California was also surprised when Lex did not charge him. And, as it happened, the gentleman was in a position to repay the kindness. His name was L.W. "Bill" Lane, owner and publisher of *Sunset*, the most prestigious and popular magazine in the West.

Soon after Lane's departure from the Rogue, Lex and DeForest were visited by a *Sunset* staff writer and photographer, both sent by Lane to do a story on the Rogue River mail boat trip for his readers. They took the trip, made notes, shot photos, and even asked the fellows when they would

Lex Fromm piloting *Skookum House*, 1948.
(Rogue River Mail Boat Trips Collection)

like to see the piece published. Lex and DeForest thought the start of the next season would be helpful. So in the June 1949 issue of *Sunset*, "The Magazine of Western Living," there appeared a detailed, four full-page feature article—one of the largest ever done by the magazine—called "Climb the Rogue River Riffles by Mail Boat." Included were nine photographs, two drawings, and two good maps. Bill Lane had repaid his boat ride.

In the 1949 season, according to the *Gold Beach Reporter*, Fromm and Sorber took over 10,000 people to Agness and back. Lex told the authors, "That June issue of *Sunset* made us go, it really put us in business." People came in droves and the fellows could not accommodate everybody using only their own boats, so they hired expert rivermen with boats big enough to carry a dozen or so passengers. Ruel Hawkins signed on with his boat, as did the Lowerys with theirs and the Thorntons with their boats.

Lex and DeForest and their crew were making two trips a day, and the Agness lunch stop, Lucas Pioneer Ranch, was serving two complete meals, one at noon and the other a couple of hours later. DeForest Sorber recalls that on some days the folks at Lucas' would run out of dishes and space to feed everyone. (In 1951, B.W. Griffitts would build a fine riverside lodge in Agness, Singing Springs Ranch, that became a popular alternate lunch stop for mail boat passengers.)

Those were good days for Lex Fromm and DeForest Sorber, the beginning of many rewarding seasons, spurred by additional magazine articles and write-ups in newspapers across the nation. They still carried the mail, and always would, but the Rogue mail boat service was now and forevermore a passenger business as well.

That season of '49, though wildly successful, consisted of long, exhausting days for the two mail boat "admirals." In addition to many

Two mail boats at the Agness landing.
(Rogue River Mail Boat Trips Collection)

The *Chinook* at Agness, June 1949.
(Rogue River Mail Boat Trips Collection)

hours of river travel, after coming in from the afternoon Agness trip one or the other of them would take the dredger boat up to clear out riffles.

The dredging operation was interesting in itself. A work boat with a winch, a long rope, and a good-sized propeller would be used to clear a riffle that had a bottom-dragging build-up of gravel. The boatman would first tie the rope to a rock or stump down below the riffle—sometimes a good distance away or across the river—and in line with the current of the riffle. With a slack line, he then positioned the dredger boat at the head of the riffle, drew the rope taut, and began revving the motor. The boat made no forward progress due to the rope holding it back, and the effect of the revved propeller churning the water was to throw back loose gravel with the prop wash. The dredge operator slowly fishtailed the boat from side to side in the channel, and at the same time moved the boat backward down the riffle by winching in the rope. The procedure caused the propeller to throw the gravel downstream as the boat inched backward, forming a channel wide enough for the next day's boats to get through. It was a tedious process and sometimes took many hours to clear one long shallow riffle.

When Lex and DeForest were not taking their turn at dredging in the evening, they worked far into the night building new mail boats in the boat shop. These were double-enders, so called because the hull came to a point

De Forest Sorber driving the 38-passenger *Skookum House*.
(Authors' Collection)

at the stern as well as at the bow. The double-ender was the common boat design on the Rogue River at that time. Soon, bright new cedar boats with names such as *Chinook* and *Crooked Riffle* and *Painted Rock* and *Copper Canyon* joined their kin at the mail boat dock of the Rogue Boat Service. One boat Lex built in 1948, *Skookum House*, was their largest to that time, with a capacity of up to thirty-eight passengers. At one time they had fourteen boats in service.

The new boats incorporated a number of Fromm design innovations, such as flatter bottoms, the fore and aft ends of which were raked, or angled, at the precise degree that would allow for maximum efficiency of water displacement and better working capability of the propeller-lift mechanism.

FROMM & SORBER: GENEROUS LIFELINES ON THE RIVER

Lex and DeForest soon earned a reputation along the river as the best, most dependable mail boat operators ever. Old-timers in Agness and Illahe recall that on numerous occasions when people upriver got sick, the fellows would come and get them. When emergency medicine was needed, Lex or DeForest would get it in Gold Beach and bring it up to a grateful, isolated river resident. If someone died in the Canyon, Lex and DeForest brought down the body, and if there was a funeral up there, and some did not have a way to get to it, a mail boat would take them. Never once was there a charge for any Samaritan service.

Some of the emergency services provided by Fromm and Sorber were courageously accomplished at night. DeForest Sorber told the authors: "Lot's of times Lex and I had to make runs to Agness at night. Pitch dark. Get someone who was sick or hurt, or needed medicine. Took a doctor up sometimes, too. You could do okay at night if you really knew the river, and we ran her every day. Even when it was dark you could see whitewater. Had to read the water and use your memory. You could do okay. It wasn't any fun though."

A number of boating mishap victims were rescued by a Rogue Boat Service craft, as well. A headline in the April 14, 1949 edition of the *Curry County Reporter* announced: "Fast Action Saves Boatmen." The article detailed the successful rescue of two men in a small boat who had run out of gas at the mouth of the Rogue. The tiny boat was being drawn out over the rough bar and was close to capsizing when someone saw them and called Fromm and Sorber.

"Lex Fromm and 'Fat' Sorber," the newspaper reported, "... with utter disregard for their own safety, took off in hasty pursuit of the periled pleasure seekers." The mail boatmen reached the doomed craft as it was

Lex Fromm loads the mail into the shore rig at Agness, circa 1948.
(Authors' Collection)

DeForest Sorber transfers mail and freight from truck to boat at the Wedderburn dock.
(Rogue River Mail Boat Trips Collection)

Mail boat arrival from Agness, Lex Fromm holding the rope, circa 1949.
(Lex Fromm Collection)

Lex Fromm coming in at Combs Lodge, 1950.
(Rogue River Mail Boat Trips Collection)

half filled with water and brought the men safely back to shore. The *Reporter* called Lex and DeForest "heroes." It was not the last time.

• • •

By 1950, the Post Office Department no longer required open bids at the end of the four-year contract. With good service the contract was always extended another four years. And Fromm and Sorber provided good service.

Also in 1950 came another Lex Fromm innovation, a radical new design well-suited to the Rogue's low water riffles. It was called a "semi-tunnel" boat. Into a large, flat-bottomed, square-stern hull was built a lengthwise recess, or large groove, in the bottom. The "tunnel" extended from the stern to about a third of the distance to the bow, then it tapered away. The propeller was inset from the rear edge of the boat, half in the tunnel and half below. In shallow water, the propeller could be raised all the way up into the tunnel and still maintain thrust by drawing water along the tunnel to the propeller blades, thereby avoiding dragging in gravel.

Lex called it a "semi-tunnel" to distinguish the design from a "full-tunnel," or tube, that was experimented with—and found inefficient—years before. The Fromm semi-tunnel boat, built especially for the Rogue,

Twin Sisters, the first semi-tunnel mail boat, 1950.
(Lex Fromm Collection)

was able to travel in only eighteen inches of water. The 1950 prototype
was named the *Twin Sisters* for a well-known rock formation in the river.
Several more semi-tunnel boats would be added to the mail boat fleet in
the years ahead.

Though passengers were the profit base of the Rogue Boat Service,
Fromm and Sorber did not neglect their primary responsibility, mail. They
had a strict policy of keeping to the mail schedule, always striving to arrive
on time. Bob Doerr recalls that never had the mail boats been on a more
dependable schedule than when Lex Fromm and Fat Sorber ran them.
"Many times," he told the authors, "those two would show up when we
didn't think they had a chance of getting through."

Freight cargo was handled promptly and efficiently, as well. On June
6, 1950, the fellows were paid a nice compliment when a group of Gold
Beach merchants took out a full-page ad in the *Reporter*:

"THANK YOU, 'UP RIVER FOLKS'

"We, the undersigned, want our many 'Up River' friends to
know that we appreciate and value most highly the business
you have given us.

" ... Your smallest orders are a pleasure to send via the excellent service given us all by the Rogue River mail boats.

(signed by numerous merchants)"

Lex and DeForest sometimes made special freight runs far into the
Canyon beyond Illahe. In 1952 Lex boated 1,800 pounds of freight through
the rapids to Andy Carr's place, just below Blossom Bar, twenty miles
upriver from Agness.

• • •

The next few years were also profitable ones for Fromm and Sorber,
with increasing numbers of passengers every season. Each spring, summer, and fall the people came, finding their way to the mail boat dock after
hearing of the trip or reading about it in magazines and newspapers. The
fellows advertised, too, promoting their scenic mail boat ride in travel
publications, newspapers, and on road signs.

According to DeForest Sorber, Lex was the outgoing member of the
partnership, the main promoter, the one who could talk to anyone—and
have them listen. Perhaps it was all those years standing in front of a
classroom. In 1953, the Champion Spark Plug Company used photos of
Lex, the boat *Crooked Riffle,* and the boat going under the Agness bridge

**Lex Fromm (foreground in white hat) relaxes at Singing Springs Ranch
before heading back downriver, circa 1953.**
(Scherbarth Collection)

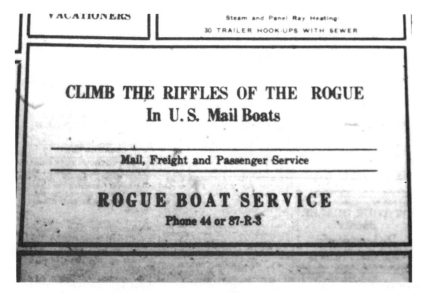

Mail boat ad, *Curry County Reporter,* **May 5, 1954.**
(Authors' Collection)

Melvin Keeler driving *Painted Rock*, 1954.
(Lex Fromm Collection)

to illustrate the advertising copy in a full-page ad published in a number of national magazines. The ad proclaimed " ... the power which keeps them on schedule is supplied by Champion Spark Plugs ... ".

• • •

Through the years, the mail boat pilots hired by Fromm and Sorber were all excellent Rogue River boatmen. There was "Mutt" Wade and Dick Wood and Hank Cooper. Ruel Hawkins drove mail boat, as did Frank Thornton, Gordon Smithers, and Dale "Spud" Johnston, Earl's boy. Fred Lowery signed on, and so did Bruce Bobo, and Melvin Keeler.

MUTT WADE REMEMBERS...

Dennis "Mutt" Wade came to the Rogue country in 1936. He quickly became an accomplished boatman, and in 1952 signed on with Fromm and Sorber as a mail boat pilot. He carried mail and passengers to Agness for twenty-two years. Today he is retired and lives on a hill overlooking the Rogue, where he can see the blue mail boats on their daily runs upriver.

Mutt Wade has a quick grin, an infectious laugh, and a great love of the Rogue. And like many old-time rivermen, he has stories.

A favorite story of Mutt's is about a rich couple and their chauffeur. "One time," said Mutt, "a long black limousine pulled up to the mail boat office. An older man and his wife got out and came on in. They had jewelry hanging all over them. They were from New York, some little town upstate, and were on a trip all over the country. They had seen the signs for the boat trip and wanted to go. I told them that would be fine and we'd be leaving shortly. Then I went outside to crank up the boat.

"I saw their uniformed chauffeur standing amongst some other customers and he was looking down at the boat. He'd look at the boat, then at the river, then at the boat again. Seemed to me he wanted to go, too. He was watching me get her all ready and I asked him if he was going on the trip. 'Oh, no,' he says, 'I have to stay and look after the car.' Well, I went back inside and asked the couple if their chauffeur was going along. They said no. I thought it didn't seem right; here's a guy hauling them all over the United States and he can't go on a little river trip—probably the best thing they'll see on their whole trip.

"So I said to them that he'd really like to go, and we talked a little bit about it, and finally they guessed it would be all right. Was he ever happy. I had a big load of folks to take up and on the way we came to a real shallow riffle that hadn't been dug, and I thought we might touch. I laced it to her up through there, but we touched a little gravel, just a little bump. The chauffeur came right up off his seat. He was the only one who knew we had touched. But he loved the whole trip, looked at everything. I hoped that after that they let him do some more things on their trip.

"That couple must have liked the mail boat trip, because over the years I took up twenty-five couples from that same town."

• • •

Mutt Wade remembers that Lex and DeForest were always willing to help anyone in trouble. "Lex and Fat were good partners," Mutt recalled. "Got along well with each other. Good boatmen, too. The best. Always trying to help someone. They went out over the river bar several times on rescues. I thought they'd drown. They won't say much about it, but both of them have saved people's lives. And if you were broke down somewhere along the river and one of them came along, well, help had arrived.

"One time I was going up with a boatload of folks. Got to a place upriver where the rudder went crazy. The rudder had a shoe under it and it went up and fastened to the bottom of the boat. (Part of the propeller-lift assembly—Authors.) Anyway, a bolt had come out of it letting it just flop around. We were pretty well stuck.

"Lex came along with his passengers and I told him what I thought it was. He took his clothes off down to his shorts—two boatloads of people

Mutt Wade gets ready to take the *Rogue* to Agness, 1957.
(Lex Fromm Collection)

Mutt Wade piloting the *Rogue*, a Fromm-built semi-tunnel boat, 1957.
(Lex Fromm Collection)

there—and went down in the water to take a look. Came back out, went to his boat, got a hammer and a bolt, and dove back under there. We could hear him hammering. Then he'd come up for air and go back down under and hammer again. Fixed her up and we were on our way."

• • •

Mutt Wade speaks highly of Lex Fromm's boat building skills. "Most of these boats around Gold Beach are patterned after Lex's," Mutt told the authors. "Some won't admit it, but its true. He's all boat builder. And I'll tell you what I've seen him do while he was building a boat. He'd sit down on a box and nail up under the deck without having to put his head down in there. He'd just nail by reaching under the deck without looking at it. Never saw anything like it."

• • •

Another Mutt Wade story has to do with Marshall Fry's last boat ride. "There was a fellow up at Agness, nice old guy named Marshall Fry. We were eating lunch at the Singing Springs mail boat drivers' table one day," Mutt recalled, "when word got around that Marshall Fry had just died. Pretty soon there was a call for Lex Fromm from Sheriff Sabin in Gold Beach. He asked Lex if he would mind bringing Marshall's body down.

Three Fromm and Sorber mail boats, circa 1950.
(Lex Fromm Collection)

Lex left us then and went down and cranked up his boat. Pretty soon he came back and, without saying anything to us, loaded up his people like we were doing.

"When the several boats of us got back down to the office and the passengers left, Lex asked a couple of us to hang around and help him with something. We went to his boat with him and he took the back seat up. There was Marshall, wrapped in a piece of canvas. We helped Lex carry him up, and just when we got right beside the office, one of Marshall's feet slipped out from under the tarp.

"Georgia, Lex's wife, was there. She looked at the foot, looked at Lex, looked at the foot again and said, 'What's that?' Lex said Marshall died and he'd brought him down. Georgia asked where he hauled him and Lex said under the back seat of the boat. Georgia said, 'You mean our customers were sitting on top of Marshall Fry?' Lex said yes, and she really hit the roof. I'll tell you she blew up. Lex was getting a kick out of it, said that's the way Marshall would have wanted to come down. So we laid him out there on the front porch and pretty soon the ambulance came for him."

Mutt could tell a thousand stories of his days on the river.

THE EAGLES NEST

In addition to their other duties, starting in the summer of 1954, Fromm and Sorber began running supplies and guests far up the Rogue beyond Illahe to Brushy Bar, where, perched on a south bank bluff sat the "Eagles Nest," the isolated fishing lodge belonging to World War II Generals Ira Eaker, Carl "Tooey" Spaatz, and Fred Anderson. Other famous generals were frequent guests: Hap Arnold, Curtis LeMay, and Nathan Twining. Ike Eisenhower was planning a visit, when he received his presidential nomination and could not come.

Lex's and DeForest's friend Ruel Hawkins had the job of ferrying the famous "Eagles" up through the whitewater to Brushy Bar in earlier years, but when he was tragically drowned in February 1954, the task fell to Fromm and Sorber. Many times those great leaders, who had guided many critical military strategies, were themselves guided by men, great in their own way, who took them safely through the chutes and cauldrons of the Rogue River rapids.

THE MAIL BOATS AND THE FLOOD OF '55

Before the construction of dams far upriver, the Rogue had a frequent propensity to flood. High, brown, roily, debris-filled water was an annual occurrence in the winter. On January 22, 1953, a photograph in the *Gold Beach Reporter* showed the mail boat office half under water, and below it was this caption: "The sign 'Ride the Riffles of the Rogue' is not very

Left to right, Generals Eaker, LeMay, and Spaatz.
(U. S. Air Force Photo)

tempting right now." It was a dangerous time to be on the river, and most boatmen stayed off. But not Lex and DeForest and their crew. They fought their way upriver and down every day that was required by the mail contract, and more often if needed in an emergency.

In January 1954, Lex made a fast trip down through high water with Mr. and Mrs. Cyril Wood of Agness. A short time after being admitted to the Curry General Hospital, Mrs. Wood gave birth to twin girls, Loretta Arlene and Loreeta Darlene. In a few days the proud parents again trusted Lex to get them safely home with their babies.

That same month the high water became a flood, and after a daring run up with the mail by DeForest Sorber came an "Agness Item" in the paper thanking him and ending with this note: "Yes, siree, 'the mail must go through,' and Fat and Lex are the boys who can do 'er."

The flood of 1955 came a few days before Christmas. Heavy snows in the Cascades, far upriver, quickly melted when unseasonable warm rains came through southern Oregon. Rivulets became creeks and creeks turned to brown torrents, emptying into an already swollen river. The Rogue rose steadily in the Canyon through Tuesday, December 20. Lex Fromm, returning from his Wednesday upriver run, reported to the newspaper that the Rogue at Agness was as high as he had ever seen it.

The mail boat office as it appeared on December 22, 1955.
(Rogue River Mail Boat Trips Collection)

The Agness suspension bridge in the flood of 1955.
(Scherbarth Collection)

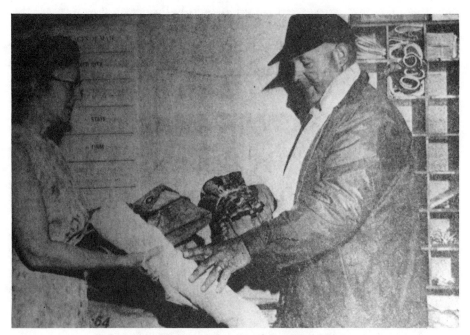

DeForest Sorber receives mail pouches from Etta Goudy,
Wedderburn postmaster, for delivery upriver, circa 1968.
(Rogue River Mail Boat Trips Collection)

According to the *Curry County Reporter*, when the river crested at about 6 a.m. on Thursday, December 22, water was running over the deck of the Agness suspension bridge which was sixty-five feet above summer flow level. In Gold Beach, Highway 101 was closed by slides. Damage was extensive all along the river. At the buildings of the Rogue Boat Service the water was nearly to the roof.

Lex and DeForest went to Agness the next day with groceries and blankets, helping where they could, taking anyone downriver who needed to go. Fromm told a reporter that the river was "just one great big long set of rapids all the way." For days they made hazardous trips up and down from Agness, dropping food off here, emergency repair materials there.

Again the mail boats had proved their value as lifelines on the Rogue; a moral obligation, willingly assumed by the partners, that went far beyond the delivery of the mail.

A CHANGE IN PARTNERS

On April 30, 1959, this item appeared on the front page of the *Curry County Reporter*: "DeForest Sorber has sold his interest in the Rogue Boat Service to Dale Johnston, who is presently one of the boat pilots ... Sorber said that he is taking over Roguewoods and will operate it as a motel this year. He will still be active with the boat service this year helping out.

"The world famous boat service carries mail from Gold Beach to Agness and also hauls about 15,000 tourists each year up the riffles of the Rogue on the 64-mile round trip."

• • •

It was a friendly parting of the partners. DeForest was just getting tired of the pace, and there were other things in life to do, including spending more time with his family. But, as happens to many in his position, DeForest's plan to "help out" for a year or so stretched on. He loved the river and he was a boatman, so he kept driving mail boat—for twenty more years.

DeForest "Fat" Sorber retired in 1979, but has never left the Rogue River and does not intend to. He fishes now, sometimes every day. And when the big blue mail boats go skimming by he will wave at them, and the passengers will wave back, most not knowing that they are passing a part of mail boat history, half of the once-famous team of Fromm and Sorber, a man who helped put the Rogue River mail boats on the map. It is believed that DeForest Sorber has made more trips up and down the Rogue River than any other boatman to this time.

CHAPTER 7

From Props To Jets

Lex's new partner, Dale "Spud" Johnston, whose nickname came from a comic strip character when he was a youth, was an able boatman who had been piloting mail boats for a number of years before becoming an associate in the business. The boat he liked to take up to Agness was a big double-ender Lex built for him in 1953, called the *Miss Agness*. She was a pretty sight, cutting up through the riffles, and Lex and DeForest previously had made advertising post cards featuring her.

For Lex Fromm, the beginning of the '60s brought continued success in the mail boat business. But it was also a time of change, a period of transition from the time-honored propeller-driven boats to a radically new method of propulsion. The modern era was about to be ushered in with something called a "jet drive."

The principle of the jet drive is easy to understand. Essentially, it is a water pump powered by an automobile engine. The jet drive creates propulsion thrust by drawing water through an intake grill in the bottom of the boat, sending it past a rotating impeller, then compressing it and shooting the water out through a nozzle behind the boat, which thrusts the boat forward. A common example of the compressed water thrust principle is a garden hose that tends to push against the hand when a heavy stream of water is forced out of a narrow nozzle opening. To steer the boat, the outtake nozzle is swiveled to the right or left, controlled by the captain's steering wheel, which causes the boat to turn in the appropriate direction.

The jet drive was a tremendous boon to Rogue River boatmen, primarily because with no propeller or rudder hanging down below the bottom of the boat they could travel through very shallow riffles, sometimes with only eight or ten inches of water in the channel. Jet drives also gave the boat unequaled maneuverability and performance.

Lex Fromm recalls that he built his first jet boat, a thirty-two passenger craft called the *Wild Horse*, in 1959. The initial jet unit Lex used was built by a man in Langlois and did not work too well, though the idea of using jets on the Rogue was sound.

In 1960 Fromm built his second jet boat, called the *Crooked Riffle*, which had two jets powered by twin Buick 280-horsepower engines. Mutt Wade drove the *Crooked Riffle*, and it was so successful that Lex built two more twin engine jet boats that year, the *Wake Up Riley* and the *Painted Rock*. As more and more passengers were showing up at the mail boat dock

Spud Johnston driving *Miss Agness*, circa 1950s.
(Rogue River Mail Boat Trips Collection)

Frank Morley's "mail dog" across from Huntley Park.
Spud Johnston piloting mail boat, circa 1959.
(Rogue River Mail Boat Trips Collection)

Berkeley jet drive unit presently on display at the mail boat office.
(Authors' Photo)

Mutt Wade coming downriver in the *Crooked Riffle*.
(Rogue River Mail Boat Trips Collection)

for the upriver ride that year, Lex and Spud kept in service their whole fleet, consisting of four jet boats, two semi-tunnels, Spud's big double-ender (the *Miss Agness*), and about half a dozen smaller double-ender boats. That winter Lex built a big jet boat, the *Copper Canyon*, that was licensed for forty-nine passengers. It was powered by three engines and three jets, the first triple jet on the Rogue.

Though Lex's jet boats were designed primarily for passengers, they still carried the mail to Agness and occasionally freight items to remote cabins upriver. Mutt Wade recalls hauling large kitchen appliances, furniture, and assorted crates on the jet mail boats to be dropped off on gravel bars along the way to Agness.

GARY COMBS COMES ABOARD

The responsibility of business ownership, with all the concerns and tedious day-to-day details, is not for everyone. So, in mid-December 1961, after two-and-a-half years, Dale "Spud" Johnston sold his half interest in the mail boat company to Gary F. Combs, grandson of well-known Rogue River resident E.E. Combs, from whom Gary learned to pilot river boats. Johnston agreed to stay on as a mail boatman and to help dredge channels and repair the boats.

As for Gary Combs, when he joined the mail boats he was home. He loved being a part of the historic boat service, felt comfortable with the customers, and became a popular guide, telling stories and pointing out interesting sites along the way to Agness.

Gary's first tourist season, in 1962, was the biggest he and Lex would see. The Seattle World's Fair was on and many more thousands of people than usual streamed up the coast highway heading for Puget Sound. And many, many of them stopped off at the mail boat dock to enjoy the famous ride to Agness. Lex and Gary were sending up all of their boats for the morning trip, and seven or eight boats went upriver each afternoon. Gary recalls that he drove every day, seven days a week, for six months, and during much of that time he made double trips. By the end of the '62 season, he knew the mail boat business intimately.

• • •

By the spring of 1964, after eighteen years at the helm of the mail boat service, Lex Fromm was ready to retire from the grind of the upriver runs. He wanted to do some traveling with his wife and spend more time building boats. It was not an easy decision for Lex, but it was time for a change of pace. So, in early June 1964, Lex sold his interest in the mail boat company to Gary Combs, with the promise to help out for awhile.

THE BIG FLOOD OF 1964: MAIL BOATS TO THE RESCUE AGAIN

By December 1964, a road was nearly completed along the south side of the Rogue River from Gold Beach to Agness. From the Agness end, a modern cement-and-steel two-way bridge had been put in across the Rogue at Coon Rock in 1962, anticipating the road from the coast. The old 1932 suspension bridge was still there, too, a couple of miles downriver from the new Coon Rock crossing. Also, there was a new span, almost completed, across the mouth of the Illinois River for the southside road to Gold Beach.

As in 1955, there had been a substantial snowpack in the Cascade and Siskiyou Mountains of southern Oregon in early December, followed by warm rains at all mountain elevations. Rain along the entire course of the Rogue was heavy and almost constant for several weeks before Christmas. It would not be a happy holiday for the river folks in 1964.

On Monday, December 21, with the river rising to flood stage, Gary Combs loaded the mail into the small winter mail boat, *Little Canyon*, and with a friend, Johnny Ricardi, started upriver on his Agness run. When they reached Lobster Creek, where the Rogue begins to narrow, they found that the water was almost to the top of massive Massacre Rock, and when they entered Little Canyon they encountered fifteen-foot swells in the current.

"We finally got into Copper Canyon," Gary told the authors, "and in there it was just awful. The boat took a wave over the stern that put about 300 gallons of water in her, enough to sink her. We quickly got that pumped out and moved on up, trying to run the eddys. We finally got to Agness and it was really getting high in there. People were waiting at the river to be sure we made it.

"After sorting the mail in the post office, we put it in the truck and started up toward Illahe. In about three miles the road was washed out. We finally got it delivered, though, and picked up the outgoing mail at Agness, then started down the river again. (It was later determined that the Rogue was rising at the rate of two feet an hour.)

"About a mile and a half downriver a kid was shooting a rifle in the air and waving. He wanted to be picked up and taken out of there, so we got him in the boat. When we got to the bottom of Little Canyon the water was washing up over a giant rock that sits by the north bank. The boat couldn't go around the rock because of thick tangles of drift, trees and such, in the water. So I ran her as fast as I could and just went over the top of the rock. We flew twenty or thirty feet beyond the rock and came down flat on the river. It was the only way to get around there. That little twenty-one-foot winter boat was a good one, a Fromm-built boat.

"The river was getting worse, so I pulled into Cameron Thom's place below Lobster Creek. They had a house on one side of the road and a guest house on the river side, way up above the water. I pulled up on the beach and ran a rope clear up to the guest house and tied it off. Got on the phone and called Lex to come and get us and the mail. I left the boat there, but on Wednesday morning it was all gone—the boat was gone and the guest house was gone. That's the only mail boat we lost in the flood."

The river rose steadily and by Tuesday, December 22, it was at full flood. The wild torrent swept through Agness, cresting at eighty-three feet above normal level. In some of the narrow places in the Canyon the water slashed between sheer rock walls, rising 125 feet above normal flow. Two dozen homes, above, below, and around Agness were swept away. The rampaging river slammed against the new Coon Rock Bridge but the solid structure held.

By Wednesday morning, the flooding Rogue had risen to where only the roof was showing at the mail boat office, and next door Lex Fromm's Wedderburn Boat Works was completely awash.

A number of riverside lodges that had come to be Rogue River landmarks in themselves were ripped from their moorings and sent turning and crumbling toward the sea. One of the river homes destroyed in the

Debris left on Coon Rock Bridge in flood of December 1964.
(Curry County Reporter Photo)

Mail boat office, December 22, 1964.
(Rogue River Mail Boat Trips Collection)

Lex Fromm's Wedderburn Boat Works as it appeared on December 22, 1964.
(Curry County Reporter Photo)

flood was the old E.E. Combs' place. "I watched my grandfather's house go right past the mail boat office," said Gary Combs. "Later when I went up there I found a toilet from his place sitting on the bank all by itself—nothing else left. It was just sitting up there about seventy-five feet above the normal water line, sitting right where the garden used to be."

• • •

The old 1932 suspension bridge collapsed during the night of Wednesday, December 23, its mangled towers and girders strewn like torn ribbons along the north bank. The almost completed bridge spanning the mouth of the Illinois, a river that had joined its bigger brother in the rampage, was also destroyed and would not be fully reconstructed for four years, though a temporary wooden low water bridge would be built to allow passage of vehicles for part of the year.

On Christmas Day the river was still at flood stage, but Lex and Gary thought they could make it up to Agness. They were concerned about the safety and condition of the upriver people in this, the greatest flood on the Rogue River in recorded history.

Illinois Bridge rubble after the 1964 flood. Fred Lowery driving the mail boat, summer 1965.
(Rogue River Mail Boat Trips Collection)

Agness suspension bridge, circa 1950.
(Scherbarth Collection)

Remains of the Agness suspension bridge after the flood of '64.
(Curry County Reporter Photo)

Georgia Fromm, Lex's wife, worried about Lex and Gary, but she had been through it before. She later said in a newspaper interview: "Those two men were all over the river, starting early on Christmas Day. There were people stranded everywhere, some of them just huddled soaking wet around the fireplace chimneys that were all that was left of their houses. They took food and medication up the river in the boats and helped move people to other homes that weren't damaged. Then they brought down a mother and her sick baby."

Bernard Jackson, owner of Cougar Lane Lodge (one of the present-day mail boat lunch stops), went upriver with Fromm and Combs that Christmas Day. He had been out of town on family business and he wanted to go up and see if his house in Agness was standing. It was still upright but there was a gigantic tree perched on the roof.

When Lex and Gary reached Agness that day all they could see was devastation. The water was down a little but not much; on the way up they had been able to touch their hands to the underside of Lobster Creek Bridge, about sixty-five feet above normal river flow. At Singing Springs Ranch only the top of the roof was showing. All of Agness was cut off.

"We came up as soon as we could," recalls Lex Fromm, "because we didn't know anything about how the people were up there. Some of them were in pretty rough shape. The caretakers at the old Crooked Riffle Lodge slept under a log the night before we got up there."

The next day, December 26, Combs and Fromm were back upriver with boatloads of food, blankets, medicine, drums of gasoline, and mail. On that day, also, they brought up Clarice Jackson, Bernard's wife, and their son, Dean.

The following day Lex and Gary went up again with more supplies and brought down twenty-one-day-old Dayleen Smithers, who was very sick, and her mother Laura. The infant was taken to Curry County Hospital where she soon recovered.

For days after the flood waters had receded, Combs and Fromm, as well as other boatmen, made the long runs to Agness, answering the needs of their upriver friends with food and supplies.

● ● ●

On February 10, 1965, Oregon Governor Mark Hatfield sent Gary Combs, as owner of the Rogue River mail boat company, a letter of thanks on behalf of the people of Oregon for the emergency assistance given by the mail boats. The governor wrote: "As an aftermath of the flood in Oregon, many stories of generosity and bravery have come to me. Perhaps among the finest is the contribution you made of your time, energy and equipment to help the people in your area as the Rogue River flooded.

The 1964 floodwaters ran over the deck of Lobster Creek Bridge.
(Authors' Photo)

The 1964 flood level sign at Singing Springs Ranch.
(Authors' Photo)

OFFICE OF THE GOVERNOR
STATE CAPITOL
SALEM 97310

February 10, 1965

MARK O. HATFIELD
GOVERNOR

Mr. Garrett F. Coombs
Wedderburn, Oregon

Dear Mr. Coombs:

As an aftermath of the flood in Oregon, many stories
of generosity and bravery have come to me. Perhaps
among the finest is the contribution you made of
your time, energy and equipment to help the people in
your area as the Rogue River flooded.

I know the people who benefited as a result of your help
are very grateful but I did want you to know that I, too,
appreciate all that you did to help prevent further
hardship for those involved.

Kindest regards and grateful thanks.

Sincerely yours,

Governor

MOH:s

Governor's letter of thanks to the mail boat company for flood assistance.
(Gary Combs Collection)

"I know the people who benefitted as a result of your help are very grateful but I did want you to know that I, too, appreciate all that you did to help prevent further hardship for those involved."

• • •

Happily, it can be reported that not one life was lost on the lower Rogue River in that flood.

• • •

Riverfolk are resilient and by the time the spring 1965 season came, much reconstruction had already been completed. The ravages of the flood were evident everywhere, though, and mail boat passengers in that season and several to follow had the opportunity to see first hand the force of a major river flood. (Still today, mail boat pilots point out high water marks on the trip and visitors can still spot giant logs perched on massive riverside rock outcroppings.)

AND THEN THERE WAS BRUCE BOBO

Among Gary Combs' mail boat pilots in the years following the '64 flood were: Mutt Wade, Fred Lowery, Dick Wood, Dale Gifford, and Ray Borders. DeForest Sorber was still driving for Gary Combs and would log thirty-six years in the mail boats, counting his Carter-Miller days, before he retired.

And then there was Bruce Bobo.

• • •

Bruce Bobo was a young man in his twenties when he came to the Rogue River after being discharged from the Army Air Corps after World War II. He married a childhood friend, Miss Inell Watson (who caught her first salmon on the Rogue with Lex Fromm at nine years of age), whose family had moved to Oregon years before from New Mexico. In 1953, Bruce and Inell opened a fishing lodge called Kimbel Kourt on the north bank of the Rogue (present site of Kimball Creek Bend Resort), east of Wedderburn.

Bruce learned to be an expert Rogue River boatman, and in 1958 signed on with Fromm and Sorber as a mail boat driver. Gary Combs, Lex Fromm, DeForest Sorber, and many river people have fond memories of Bruce Bobo, who drove for Gary until 1976. (He passed away shortly thereafter from cancer.)

Bruce Bobo was a character. His daughter, Laurie Wills, now on the office staff at the mail boat company, recalled some stories for the authors.

Bruce was a big husky fellow, gentle and shy. He was quiet around strangers on land, but when he was on the mail boat he really opened up.

Bruce Bobo.
(Laurie Wills Collection)

He liked to entertain the folks, as the boat pilots do today, and put on a little show for them with stories and jokes on the way up-river. And once in awhile he was not beyond pulling a prank on his passengers. Like the incident with Cy Wood...

Cyril "Cy" Wood was a veteran Rogue fishing guide and a friend of Bruce. Whenever Cy and Bruce met on the river, Cy in his small fishing boat and Bruce in the big blue mail boat, each would point their finger at the other and "shoot" instead of waving. One day, when Bobo was stopped in an eddy along the shore showing his people an animal, Cy happened by in his boat. The passengers watched Bruce point his finger and "shoot" Cy. Then Cy pointed and shot Bruce. But this time when he was shot, Bruce fell down on the pilot's deck of the mail boat! Down and dead in the middle of an eddy on the Rogue River. Some of the people gasped and some laughed and some just stared, and when Bruce figured he had played it out he got up and continued his narration as if nothing had happened. The relieved passengers loved it.

Another time, Larry Lucas, proprietor of Lucas Pioneer Ranch, had given Bruce a big box of bell peppers to take down for the folks at the mail boat office. Lucas was always doing that, sending lots of good Agness produce to friends downriver. But bell peppers happened to be a weakness of Bruce Bobo. So, when he started back down from Agness with his passengers, he picked a nice pepper out of the box to sort of munch on as they went. Then he would tell a story. And have another bell pepper. Then he would stop so the folks could take pictures of a bear or deer. And each time he would get another pepper out of the box. Bruce ate so many delicious Agness bell peppers by the time the mail boat reached the dock that, according to his daughter, he never touched another one for twenty years.

Laurie said that Bruce used to keep a trip log each season; notations of weather, animals seen, passenger counts, and so forth. She said that one afternoon he came home looking especially pleased. The family asked him about it and he said his trip log showed that on that day he took his 10,000th passenger to Agness. Laurie recalls that her father got a little choked up and quietly said, "I've taken 10,000 people up and back safely." He was proud of that.

• • •

Even after vehicles were driving freely into Agness the mail continued to be carried by the mail boats. By 1968 the temporary low water bridge over the mouth of the Illinois River had been replaced by a high, permanent span, allowing vehicular traffic into Agness and Illahe by the Gold Beach road all year. The old canyon-hugging road over the mountains from Agness to Powers, put in by the CCC boys in 1937, was passable much of the year, too. But still the mail came by way of mail boats.

DeForest Sorber remembers a day, after the Gold Beach road was opened, when one of his passengers happened to be a United States postal inspector, who rode up on the mail boat for a routine check of the Agness post office. As Sorber and the postmaster were sorting the mail, the inspector asked the postmaster good-naturedly when they expected to start bringing the mail by road. DeForest told the authors: "The postmaster looked at him kinda funny, and said, 'We aren't putting it on the road. There isn't a contract mail truck outfit anywhere with as good a record for dependability as these mail boats. They have served the people well up here, and they're part of the history up here, and we're sure not about to change now'."

• • •

Under the ownership of Gary Combs, the mail boats continued to provide excellent mail and passenger service as they had in the past. As the '60s made way for a new decade, the fame of the Rogue River mail boats was spread even wider by satisfied customers, as well as through additional feature articles in magazines, including: *Life, National Geographic,* and *Sunset.* Many newspaper travel editors and writers also rode the riffles of the Rogue with Combs and his crew, writing about the picturesque trip in over forty newspapers from across the nation, including: New York, Chicago, Philadelphia, Miami, Kansas City, Dallas, Denver, and Los Angeles. The Rogue River mail boats were being indelibly marked on America's recreation map.

CHAPTER 8

Continuing The Tradition: The Mail Boats Today

A MAN NAMED KAMMER

In the summer of 1970, a young college graduate returned home to Gold Beach, and he wanted to be a mail boat pilot. His name was Ed Kammer. Ed had grown up on the Rogue River and had learned to run his father's fishing boat when he was ten. Two years later Ed built his first river boat, with his father's help, and for his eighth grade graduation his dad gave him a sixteen-foot river boat. "I ran around all over the Rogue with it," Ed told the authors. "It was an outboard and getting up to Agness with no propeller-lift was pretty tricky, so I had to learn the river really well."

After obtaining his pilot's license, Kammer worked for Combs that summer of 1970 driving the big passenger mail boats, and liked it. When the season ended, Gary kept the hardworking young man with him as the winter mail carrier boating mail to Agness three times a week. Ed also worked in the shop as a mechanic, getting the boats ready for the next season.

In the fall of 1971, Ed married Sue Lind, a pretty medical technologist from Klamath Falls, whom he had met when they both attended college there.

After several years of driving mail boat and handling the company's maintenance program, Ed branched out into his own business. In the winter of 1974-75, he had a twenty-nine-foot aluminum-hulled boat built that would carry thirty passengers. He installed twin 225-horsepower Chrysler engines and two Berkeley jet drives in the boat, and called it the *Osprey*. In the spring of 1975, arranging with Gary Combs to use the mail boat office and dock, Ed began offering to carry passengers in the *Osprey* on a thrilling 104-mile round-trip into the federally designated "Wild" portion of the Rogue River.

Ed's trip went twenty miles beyond Agness—fifty-two miles into the Rogue Canyon—to the foot of the infamous Blossom Bar, the boulder-choked rapids that serves as the end of the line for powerboats. The trip took people far beyond roads and civilization, up into the wild reaches of the Rogue. Passengers of Ed's Mail Boat UpRiver Trips company went to Agness, where they stopped for a rest at Singing Springs Ranch. Then,

Mail boat office, 1975.
(Rogue River Mail Boat Trips Collection)

Ed Kammer on the *Osprey* coming through Half Moon Bar Rapids, 1975.
(Rogue River Mail Boat Trips Collection)

instead of turning back downriver as did the regular mail boats, Ed proceeded further upriver to the turnaround at Blossom Bar. On the way down, Ed stopped at a remote Canyon lodge where his passengers had lunch, after which they reboarded the *Osprey* for the equally thrilling downriver trip.

Though the 1975 season proved to be a success for Ed's whitewater venture, it was something new for the mail boat service, and not every day was the thirty-passenger *Osprey* filled. So that winter Ed built a smaller, twelve-passenger boat, the *Otter*, that he planned to use for lighter loads the next season.

Fortunately, he rarely had to use the smaller boat, for with advertising promotion and the spreading of good words by happy customers, the 104-mile trip grew rapidly in popularity. It was a fun, comfortable, exciting—and safe—way for people to experience the wilderness world of the Rogue Canyon.

The complete safety of the ride was emphasized. No Kammer boat ever wrecked on the long trip and no passenger was ever hurt. (The company's safety record remains unblemished to this day.) Young and elderly alike could take the whitewater journey with ease, as did Miss Minnie Lady, who, at ninety, was one of Ed's most senior citizens in the early days of the 104-mile "Wild Water Trip," as it was then known.

Stan Wade taking the *Rogue* into Two Mile Rapids.
(Rogue River Mail Boat Trips Collection)

In 1976 Ed Kammer signed Stan Wade to pilot the 104-mile trip, allowing himself more time to promote the business and continue helping Gary Combs with the mail boats. Stan, nephew of Mutt Wade, was an excellent boatman and a natural for the long trip because he loved the upper river and was actively interested in the Rogue's natural and human history.

ED AND SUE KAMMER: ROGUE RIVER MAIL BOAT TRIPS, INC.

By 1980 Gary Combs was ready for a slower pace and as a major step in that regard, he sold the mail boat business in its entirety to Ed and Sue Kammer, effective December 1 of that year.

Like other longtime mail boat operators before him, Gary stayed on with the new owners to help out and drive mail boats. (Gary Combs is still a mail boat pilot, and at the time of this writing has logged almost thirty years on the blue boats—second only to DeForest Sorber's thirty-six years.)

Ed and Sue Kammer took over the helm of the mail boat company with the same high enthusiasm that they approach all aspects of their life. Like any successful business, the mail boat enterprise took a lot of time and work, which the Kammers were willing to give. For special assistance, Lex Fromm, grandmaster of boat building and the Rogue River, was always close by, lending experienced hands when needed, offering good advice when asked.

The Kammers infused the mail boat company with a freshness and vitality that spurred an even wider popularity of the famous blue boats. They built a large, appealing office and spacious gift shop (open all year), where passengers can enjoy complimentary coffee or tea while waiting to board the upriver boats. They developed new promotional ideas, pursued and established a bus-tour trade for their business. The mail boat trips are now a featured stop on many organized bus tours traveling the United States.

In June 1983 Ed and Sue sent a full size mail boat inland to the Oregon Expo near Medford, where free rides were given on an adjacent lake. And in 1986 they participated in a display in the Oregon Pavilion at Expo '86 in Vancouver, British Columbia.

● ● ●

A new upriver trip was established by the mail boat company in 1983 that has proven highly popular. For those wishing to go farther than the original 64-mile round-trip to Agness, but not the entire distance of the 104-mile wilderness whitewater run to Blossom Bar and back, the Kammers began an 80-mile whitewater tour that goes eight miles beyond

The present mail boat office.
(Authors' Photo)

Rogue River Mail Boat Trips gift shop and passenger lobby.
(Authors' Photo)

Tim Arntzen piloting the *Rogue* on the 80-mile trip.
(Rogue River Mail Boat Trips Collection)

**Ed Kammer stands beside the 63-passenger *Golden Eagle*, built in 1983,
the first boat on the Rogue River licensed to carry over 49 people.**
(Rogue River Mail Boat Trips Collection)

Agness. The 80-mile boats blend the pleasures of the shorter scenic trip with the excitement of the longer wilderness run. On the 80-mile journey passengers have the opportunity to experience Rogue River whitewater by climbing through Shasta Costa, Two Mile, Old Diggins, Little Wildcat, Foster and Watson Creek Rapids, before turning around at the top of historic Big Bend.

The mail boat fleet was enlarged in 1983 by the addition of the *Golden Eagle*, a forty-three-foot boat powered by three engines and triple jets, able to carry sixty-three passengers. She was the first boat on the Rogue licensed by the U.S. Coast Guard for over forty-nine people.

In 1985 the mail boat company celebrated its 90th anniversary—1895 to 1985—and every ninetieth passenger rode free. Also in that year Gold Beach hosted a meeting of fifty Oregon postmasters, who enjoyed immensely a trip on the U.S. Mail boats. And in June of 1985, the *Wildcat* was introduced. Launched on June 9 to be used primarily on the long 104-mile trip, the *Wildcat* was the first triple engine, three jet craft to be used in the upper section of the Canyon. The *Wildcat*, a forty-two-passenger boat, can skim through only six inches of water and develops 1,020-horsepower, a far cry from the old 5- to 12-horsepower motors of the early mail boats.

Stan Wade plowing through Clay Hill Rapids in the *Wildcat*, 1985.
(Rogue River Mail Boat Trips Collection)

As the business continued to grow through the '80s, new ideas and new boats kept coming. In 1986 the phrase "Mail Yourself Upriver" was born, and the three trips took on new identities in ads and brochures: the original 64-mile trip became "Postage Due, Agness, Oregon"; the 80-mile tour was "Special Delivery"; and the 104-mile trip was called "Handle With Care."

Rogue River mail boat history was made in 1986 in two respects. The first wedding ever held on a mail boat was performed on board the *Golden Eagle* at Tom East Riffle, twenty-four miles upriver. The happy couple were Rebecca Soward, a mail boat company employee, and Grant Hawman. Also that year the first female mail boat pilot was hired, Janine Smith, who had taken her first ride on a mail boat when she was five.

In 1987, the *Rogue Queen* was built, another first for the Rogue River. Designed by Ed Kammer and boat builder Wayne Adams, the forty-three-foot, eighty-passenger, glass enclosed tour boat was built in Adams' Sea People Manufacturing boat shop. The big tri-jet *Queen* can travel in ten inches of water and is used on the Agness run during inclement weather and by large tour groups. The *Rogue Queen* is the only glass enclosed jet tour boat known to exist in the United States.

The "Champagne Cruise" is a popular attraction that originated with the launching party for the *Rogue Queen*. The late afternoon-evening river cruise to Agness is scheduled on weekends from July 1 through Labor Day. Champagne, soft drinks, and snacks are served along the way, with dinner at Agness. The hostesses for the cruise are from the mail boat office staff. There is also a special "Mother's Day Champagne Cruise."

Another unique cruise attraction, "Dixieland on the Rogue," began on July 4, 1988. An idea proposed by staff member Cynthia Kuhlman, "Dixieland on the Rogue" has been held every year since, for one day on or near Independence Day. This popular excursion features a trip to Agness, where at Cougar Lane Lodge the passengers are treated to a lively concert by the Oregon Jazz Band and an old-fashioned barbecue dinner.

The 1989 season began an annual tradition of a distinctive tour group, the tribal elders of the Siletz Indians. It was the ancestors of the Siletz people who were taken from the Rogue Canyon in 1856, after the Rogue River Indian War, and placed on a coastal reservation to the north. Now the people return to the Rogue each summer, chartering a mail boat for a trip to Agness, where they spend a night or two recalling their legacy and sharing stories handed down from their forefathers about life on the great river.

The launching of a new mail boat, the *Rogue* opened the 1989 season. By the next year, Rogue River Mail Boat Trips had nine boats in the fleet, including another brand-new one, the *Wake Up Riley*, which is licensed to

The largest and the smallest of the mail boat fleet: *Rogue Queen* **and** *Otter*.
(Authors' Photo)

Siletz Indians on their 1990 mail boat trip to Agness.
(Rogue River Mail Boat Trips Collection)

The *Rogue Queen* on the original 64-mile mail boat trip.
(Rogue River Mail Boat Trips Collection)

The *Wake Up Riley*, the 88-passenger 1990 addition to the mail boat fleet.
(Authors' Photo)

carry eighty-eight passengers. The *Wake Up Riley* is forty-three feet long
and fourteen feet wide, as is the *Rogue Queen*, the maximum size allowed
on the river.

Among the newer boats, *Wildcat, Golden Eagle, Rogue Queen, Rogue,*
and *Wake Up Riley,* were also the *Osprey* and the *Otter,* from Ed Kammer's
early whitewater trip. Included in the mail boat fleet, and used regularly,
are the last two wooden boats, both built by Lex Fromm. The *Chinook* is
a twin engine, twin jet, forty-nine passenger craft built in Lex's Wedderburn Boat Works around 1971. The other wooden boat is the *Blue Heron,*
constructed by the venerable boat builder in 1977. (As of 1990, Lex
estimates that he has produced about 300 boats, including a number of
large ocean-going fishing vessels.)

There is a third Fromm-built boat used by the mail boat company as a
dredger. This "digger" boat, a thirty-foot double-ender, was built by Lex
Fromm in 1951 for E.E. Combs, grandfather of Gary Combs. Years ago it
was fitted with a riffle-dredging winch and is presently used for that
purpose by Gordon Smithers. The old boat is a popular curiosity among
visitors, who enjoy viewing a rare example of an historic boat design. It
is called the "E.E.," and is the last double-ender still afloat on the Rogue
River.

The *Wake Up Riley* uses three Hamilton jets.
(Authors' Photo)

The *Wake Up Riley* is powered by three Ford engines.
(Authors' Photo)

Repainting of all the mail boats is done each winter by Jon Hockema.
(Authors' Photo)

For safety and maintenance, all of the boats are taken out of the water at season's end and put under cover. Work is done on them all winter by mechanic Bob Alexander, including engine and jet drive overhaul and parts replacement. In addition, all of the boats are given a fresh coat of "mail boat blue" paint by mail boat pilot Jon Hockema.

Another important factor in the development of the mail boat company has been the support staff—the cheerful ladies who greet the passengers and keep hundreds of reservations in order.

Sue Kammer and her assistant, Cynthia Kuhlman, who joined the company in June 1987, work with a staff of twelve to fifteen during the season. The office and gift shop are open all year for phone and in-person reservations. The staff includes students, a former mail boat pilot's daughter, a talented poetess who writes poems for the company's newsletter (See Chapter 9), and the Kammer's daughter, Jenny, who wants to follow her father and become a Rogue River pilot. The Rogue River mail boat experience always begins with a warm smile and a friendly greeting.

THE MAIL BOAT PILOTS

The mail boat pilots of today are an experienced, safety-conscious crew, licensed by the U.S. Coast Guard, and knowledgeable about river

The Rogue River mail boat pilots and staff. Front: (left to right) Judy Biesen, Claudia Martin, Susan Kelly, Megan Downer, Beth Turner, Shannon Sprague, Rebecca Soward-Hawman, Jodie Sprague, Jenny Kammer, Cynthia Kuhlman. Back Row: Tim Arntzen, Jon Hockema, Stan Wade, Hugh McGinnis, Scott Adams, Gary Combs, Jim Sorber. Standing: Sue Kammer, Ed Kammer, Bob "Santa Claus" Alexander. 1990 Christmas photo. (*Rogue River Mail Boat Trips Collection*)

The venerable old "E.E.," a 1951 Fromm-built double-ender,
now used as a dredger by the mail boat company.
(Authors' Photo)

Gordon Smithers dredging a shallow riffle above Lobster Creek Bridge.
(Rogue River Mail Boat Trips Collection)

history and wildlife. They are of this time, but are tied by tradition and the river to the mail boatmen of the past, showing the same respect and dedication to the Rogue and the people they serve.

Entertaining narrators as well as skilled rivermen, the pilots who handle the blue boats are a major part of the Rogue River mail boat trip experience.

GARY COMBS

Veteran mail boat pilot Gary Combs has been driving for nearly thirty years and has a long history on the Rogue. He owned the mail boat company from 1962 until 1980, when he chose a quieter way of life. Gary's way with a story makes him a popular mail boat driver.

Through the years he has had many unique experiences, including a big fish story.

Gary was bringing his passengers down from Agness on an afternoon trip, entering Copper Canyon about dusk. "I always idle down through there because it's so pretty that time of evening and my passengers like to take pictures," Gary recalls. "All of a sudden, there was a tremendous splash and a thump on the bow. Water was everywhere and the windshield was broken. Here was this huge sturgeon laying on the bow and beginning to slide off into the river.

"You know, a sturgeon will come up out of the water and flop over sideways. Well, he did and landed right across the bow. A lady in the front seat was standing up screaming and trying to crawl up and over the back of the seat.

"I was so startled that when I got on the speaker all I could say was, 'That was a sturgeon, folks!' The passengers slowly settled down, and I asked the lady up front why she had been screaming like that and so scared. 'Oh,' she said, 'all I could think of was Jaws!'

"I imagine that big old fish looked like Jaws to her. They're real strange, monster-looking things. That's the first time that's happened and probably the last."

STAN WADE

A native of Gold Beach, Stan followed in the wake of his uncle, Mutt Wade, when he became a mail boat pilot. The authors asked Stan if he had carried any celebrities, and he replied: "To me any person that's eighty-five years old, or over, is a celebrity. And we have a lot of them that age. I always tell my passengers when we have a 'celebrity' on board."

Called "Eagle Eye" by his passengers for his ability to spot eagles, osprey, and other wildlife on the mail boat trip, Stan has been a favorite driver for fifteen years. People return year after year and ask to ride "Stan's boat," the *Wildcat.*

The first day Stan drove the 104-mile trip was the day Ed and Sue Kammer's daughter, Jenny, was born. According to Sue, Stan will never forget how long he has been driving because each year on her birthday, Jenny reminds him.

JIM SORBER

Jim is a second generation mail boat pilot, son of DeForest "Fat" Sorber. "I always say I have river water in my veins," said Jim Sorber. "I grew up on the river; it's always there even though it changes."

On a fall day in 1990, Jim Sorber was on the mail run to Agness, as he has been for eleven years, when he spotted two small bear cubs swimming across the Rogue. He slowed the boat and moved closer so his passengers could watch, but not close enough to frighten the young cubs. Meanwhile, he was scanning the river banks looking for the mother bear. Suddenly, she charged out from the bushes, reared up on her hind legs, and headed into the water straight for the boat. Not wanting to cause the mother bear unnecessary concern, he quickly moved the boat away and continued upstream.

The mail boat pilots are considerate of and protect the wildlife along the Rogue River Canyon. They always make a point of telling their passengers that the mail boats and its visitors are guests in the home country of the wildlife.

TIM ARNTZEN

The Arntzen family moved to Gold Beach from San Jose, California when Tim was one-and-a-half years old. He grew up on the river at his father's north bank resort, where his dad was a fishing guide. "I would ride along as bait boy for no pay, but my reward sometimes was that Dad would sit me up in his lap and kind of let me drive the boat home."

Tim's ties to the Rogue continued to grow, and even though he is now an attorney, he only practices law in the winter. In the summer Tim drives mail boats as he has for nine years.

Tim Arntzen's most harrowing river encounter occurred a few years ago on the 80-mile whitewater trip. At Big Bend the mail boat must use a shallow, narrow channel on the north side of a gravel bar island because of solid bedrock on the south side. Once the pilot starts through this channel, he needs to keep up speed to navigate the low water, and cannot stop for any reason because of the shallowness.

One day, when Tim and his passengers were coming around the gravel bar island, they surprised a young woman who was sunbathing on the gravel bar. She had been "skinny dipping" and stretched out in the sun to get warm. As the mail boat entered the channel, the lady panicked—her clothes were on the north bank and there were no bushes on the island for her to hide behind.

She took off wading the river right in front of the mail boat. Tim slowed down as much as he could, ready to stop, though the boat and passengers would be stuck on the bottom of the channel until help arrived. He hoped she was fast. She was.

HUGH McGINNIS

The McGinnis family lived in the Agness area, and though Hugh was born in the Gold Beach hospital, he did not come back downriver until he was ten years old.

Hugh was raised on Oak Flat, near the confluence of the Rogue and Illinois Rivers. He was already an experienced young boatman when, after the '64 flood, he had to row back and forth across the Rogue to attend school. Hugh began guiding fishermen when he was sixteen years old and obtained his passenger boat license at eighteen. He has been driving mail boat for the Kammers for six years, usually on the 80-mile whitewater trip.

Hugh likes to joke with his passengers. One time he was telling the folks that the turkey vultures count heads in his boat as he passes upriver. He said if somebody is missing coming down on the return trip, the turkey vultures fly upstream for a look. "We were going upriver, and not ten minutes had passed," Hugh recalled, "when the mail boat came around a bend and there sat a turkey vulture pulling on an old dirty shirt. Everybody laughed except one lady—she thought it was real and wanted me to go back."

Another turkey vulture story has to do with "river justice." Several years ago, a passenger was having a terrible time. She didn't like the wind; she didn't like her seat; she didn't like the river, the lunch, or the wildlife. She had complained about everything up and back. The other passengers were becoming annoyed and Hugh admits it had been a rough trip.

Coming downriver, he stopped the boat so the passengers could watch some turkey vultures and a snowy white egret standing behind them on a gravel bar. The unhappy lady was sitting in the middle of the front seat, voicing her opinion of the turkey vultures.

Just then the egret flew over the turkey vultures and startled them, causing them to take off over the bow of the boat. One turkey vulture relieved himself as he passed over the boat, and down it came, landing right in the grouchy lady's lap.

A forced, polite silence fell over the passengers. Hugh wet a towel in the river and passed it to the red-faced woman. He remembers she was quiet for the rest of the trip after her encounter with "river justice."

JON HOCKEMA

A native of Curry County, Jon was born and raised in the Pistol River area, about twelve miles south of the Rogue. Jon's great-great-grandfather on his mother's side was chief of the Coquille tribe and his mother's grandmother was Cherokee. His grandfather in Pistol River was a full-blooded Dutchman. Jon says, "It's kind of unique, a mix of Coquille, Cherokee, and Dutch. Quite a crazy mixture." At six feet, seven inches tall, Jon's height is not what impresses the visitor; it is his easy, soft-spoken, dignified manner.

His favorite mail boat story is of the eastern gentleman and the bear.

Jon once had a passenger who spoke with a pronounced Boston accent. He sat in front of the pilot's console and during the trip sipped whiskey from tiny airplane-size bottles. "All the way up the river he's wanting to see a 'beah'," Jon recalls. "He's got to see a 'beah'. He's looking for 'beah' all the time.

"We get to Agness and I drop people off for lunch at Lucas, Cougar Lane, and last Singing Springs. He wasn't interested in having anything to eat, he was having a good time. So I went up to lunch.

"Across from Singing Springs is an open pasture on a hill, where cattle graze. He sat on the dock drinking and looking at the field. I came down the trail from lunch and he says, 'Oh, Johnny. Oh, Johnny, I seen the most beautiful beah.' He's all excited.

"Now it is not impossible to see a bear right there in the Agness area, so I asked him if he was sure. 'Oh, yes. It came out on that hillside and walked right across,' he said. 'Oh, it was a big, shiny, beautiful black beah, the biggest most beautiful beah you've ever seen. I took pictures of it.'

"One of the passengers took me aside and he says, 'Jon, it was a black Angus cow. None of us had the heart to tell him he'd seen a cow, he was enjoying his bear so much.'

"I don't know, when he developed his film, if he realized his 'big, shiny, beautiful black beah' wasn't."

SCOTT ADAMS

Mail boat pilot Scott Adams is the great-grandson of pioneers John and Sadie Adams, whose upriver Potato Illahe Ranch has long been a Rogue River landmark. Scott's father, Wayne, built and helped design the mail boat *Rogue Queen.*

As a young boy, Scott used to watch the mail boats go by. He wanted to be a pilot, but never thought it would happen. "You grow up on the river and the river is your life. Piloting is different, and it's a very rare job. I love it. Even when I get a day off, I go get in our private boat and head upstream."

He recently took a group of passengers from South America on a special cruise. Though none except their translator spoke English, they enjoyed the river scenery and wildlife, but Scott was not sure they understood his jokes.

On another trip Scott was showing his passengers a Western pond turtle sunning on a rock. One lady was sure the turtle was stuffed and would not believe it was alive. Nothing Scott could say would change her mind. She finally was convinced, however, when the turtle jumped into the water.

• • •

All of the mail boat pilots agree they would not be content away from the river. They love what they do, they enjoy the people, and each in his own way is a showman, giving the mail boat passengers a wonderful time on the unique Rogue River.

DO THE MAIL BOATS STILL CARRY THE MAIL?

Without doubt, the most often asked question of the mail boat pilots and office staff in modern times is: "Do the 'mail' boats still really carry the mail?"

The answer is an unqualified, "Yes."

All upriver mail of every kind—including parcel post—is taken up by the mail boat company, per four-year renewable contract. Seasoned mail boat pilot Jim Sorber, son of DeForest Sorber, is the mail carrier from May 1 through October 31. Jim begins his mail days (every day except Sunday) by picking up the upriver mail at the Gold Beach post office. Then he proceeds to the boat dock, where he loads the mail onto his boat, usually the *Golden Eagle*, or in rainy weather the *Rogue Queen*. After preparing the boat and welcoming his passengers aboard, Jim starts up the river. There are still a few residents along the river between Gold Beach and Agness who request their mail to be dropped off at their private docks, and Jim obliges.

Upon arriving at Agness, Sorber lets his passengers off at the lodge of their choice for lunch, then he ties up at the Lucas Pioneer Ranch dock where the 4-wheel drive mail truck is parked. Loading the sacks and cartons of Agness and Illahe mail into the rig, he heads for the Agness post office, where he sorts the mail with the help of Postmaster Sandy Stallard. Three days a week Jim also runs a twenty-five-mile route with the mail

Jim Sorber at Agness unloading mail from the *Rogue Queen*.
(Authors' Photo)

Jim Sorber sorting mail at the Agness post office.
(Authors' Photo)

Waiting for the day's passengers.
(Authors' Photo)

Ed and Sue Kammer on the mail boat dock with Lex Fromm.
(Authors' Photo)

truck, after which he returns to the post office and picks up the outgoing mail for transportation downriver to the Gold Beach post office.

Then Jim grabs a quick lunch, when he can, and heads back to his boat with the mail, leaving the mail truck at the landing. After picking up his passengers, the "water route mailman" starts downriver.

During the winter months, the Agness-Illahe mail is taken up three days a week.

Yes, the mail boats still deliver the mail.

THE TRADITION—KEEPING THE FLAME ALIVE

The Rogue River mail boat company is one of only two rural mail carriers still delivering the mail by boat on rivers in the United States.

Though passengers are the mainstay of their business, Ed and Sue Kammer value and respect the historic tradition of the Rogue River mail boats. They recognize and accept the responsibility inherent in the fact that their boats are direct, lineal descendants of Elijah Price's and Henry Moore's first 1895 mail boat. Their pilots can now skim with relative ease over the same riffles that required backbreaking work with the pike pole in earlier times. But the contract the Kammers hold from the U.S. Postal Service is essentially the same one fought for and won by such Rogue River luminaries as Johnny Woodworth, Elihu Fry, Frank "Old Reliable" Lowery, Roy Carter, and Lex Fromm and DeForest Sorber. And the mandate is the same: Deliver the U.S. Mail to the people of the Rogue River Canyon.

The torch was passed in 1980, and the flame is still alive. It is a responsibility Ed and Sue Kammer treasure.

CHAPTER 9

A Memorable Experience: The Rogue River Mail Boat Trip

From deep inside the mountains,
Through canyons and forests to the sea;
A memory of riding the Rogue River,
Is where my thoughts will be.

Rebecca Soward-Hawman

For those who have experienced a Rogue River mail boat trip, this section on the history of the river sites, riffles, creeks, and rapids will invoke fond memories. For the reader who has not been on the blue boats, the following capsule descriptions of interesting places along the way are a preview of what awaits the first time mail boat passenger.

Rogue River Mail Boat Trips offers a choice of three round-trip excursions on sleek, safe, comfortable hydrojets: the original 64-mile mail run to Agness; an 80-mile whitewater trip; and a 104-mile wilderness journey to Blossom Bar, as far up the Rogue as powerboats can navigate. Anyone, whether young or elderly, athletic or physically limited, can enjoy a mail boat hydrojet ride.

Mail boat trips up the Rogue provide the unique adventure of being totally absorbed into a natural environment. As the boat glides smoothly into the Canyon, the pilot skillfully threading through the riffle-dotted channel, the spirit soaks in the experience, the sense of place. The eye seeks to catch it all—the fast water, the deep pools, details on shore, an eagle or osprey overhead.

Occasionally, the boat will slow as hushed passengers watch deer feeding at the water's edge, or a bear prowling the shore, or a comical family of otters swimming and playing their way along in the shoreline shallows. At such times the stillness of the Rogue Canyon surrounds and soothes the travelers, infusing them with a peaceful contentment that has lured many visitors back again and again. Then the boat continues on and the wind rushes by, refreshing and quickening the senses, heightening the anticipation of what might lay around the next bend.

Some of the place names on the Rogue River honor long gone pioneers, others are of more recent vintage. Some mark the sites of significant incidents on the river, and a few have humorous origins.

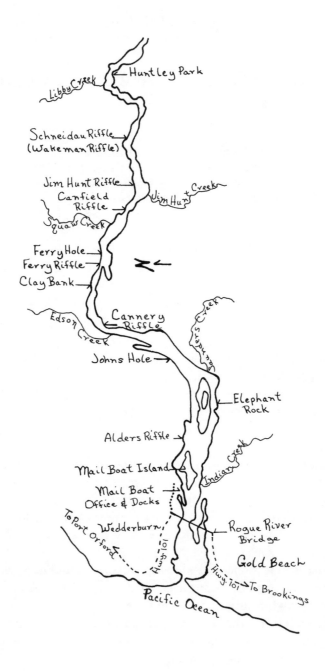

So come along on an armchair mail boat journey, traveling the historic water path of Price, Lowery, and Fromm, into the isolated, rugged wilderness reaches of the Rogue River Canyon.

The adventure begins at the mail boat dock.

MAIL BOAT OFFICE AND DOCKS

The mail boat office and gift shop is located on the historic site of R.D. Hume's north bank cannery, which was built in 1895. Hume established the company town of Wedderburn, including the Bay View Hotel, and the world famous cannery. Through the years, Wedderburn has maintained its own separate identity from Gold Beach.

The beautiful two-story mail boat office and gift shop is built of specially milled vertical-grain redwood. Designed in 1983 by Ed Kammer, it utilizes skylights and tiles to take advantage of solar power.

After checking in for the trip, passengers may browse through the gift shop, enjoy complimentary coffee or tea, and anticipate the day's adventure.

Tied up at the sturdy Douglas fir docks, which stretch 350 feet, is the mail boat fleet, with familiar Rogue country names: *Chinook, Blue Heron, Osprey, Otter, Wildcat, Golden Eagle, Rogue, Wake Up Riley,* and the unique glass enclosed *Rogue Queen.* Following the boarding of one of these boats and placing lunch orders with the mail boat pilot, the hydrojet slides gracefully away from the dock.

ISAAC PATTERSON MEMORIAL BRIDGE

Formally named for Isaac Lee Patterson, Oregon's eighteenth governor, it is more commonly called the Rogue River Bridge. Built by state bridge Engineer C.B. McCullough using the prestressed-concrete Freyssinet technique, developed by a French engineer-inventor, the bridge was dedicated in May 1932. Its length is 1,898 feet. There is a twin to this bridge in France. The distinctive arches spanning the mouth of the Rogue River present a picturesque view to Oregon Coast visitors.

The blue hydrojet now turns and begins its upstream journey.

INDIAN CREEK

R.D. Hume's original cannery and company town was built here. A mile up Indian Creek, Hume operated a salmon hatchery, the forerunner of today's aquaculture. On the night of October 19, 1893, the cannery and town burned to the ground under mysterious circumstances. Rumors around Gold Beach suspicioned Hume's arch rival, the Alaska Packers Association, although the mystery was never solved. Two years later

The *Golden Eagle* from the pilot's perspective.
(Rogue River Mail Boat Trips Collection)

Hugh McGinnis piloting the *Golden Eagle*, Rogue River Bridge in background.
(Authors' Photo)

Hume established the town of Wedderburn on the north bank and rebuilt his cannery.

MAIL BOAT ISLAND

Across from Indian Creek to the north is Mail Boat Island, a popular nesting place for the American bald eagle. Frequently seen in this area are harbor seals, Steller sea lions, and California sea lions, drawn here by the abundance of fish. Also, an occasional whale will come into the estuary; Sue Kammer remembers one in early May 1982. The whale was about twenty-five feet long and spent the day in the water between the mail boat docks and the island.

ALDERS RIFFLE

Alders Riffle was a famous drift for commercial fishermen on the Rogue until 1935, when commercial fishing was banned on the river by state legislation. The riffle was named in the early days for the lush alders that grew along the river banks, but the trees were washed away in the 1964 flood. Of two original riffles, only one can be seen at low tide during the fall.

ELEPHANT ROCK

Located about one mile upstream, this mammoth river monolith was named by the crew of the schooner *Samuel Roberts* in 1850. While the *Roberts* was anchored in the Rogue River, her crew went exploring and carved the date and the ship's initials in the rock. Though the river at one time ran freely around Elephant Rock, today only at high tide or during winter water is the rock separated from its midstream island. The top of the rock is a nesting site for great blue heron.

SAUNDERS CREEK

German immigrant John A. Sannders settled at the mouth of this creek. Through a common misspelling of his last name, the creek is called Saunders. He built a grist mill near the mouth of the stream shortly after the Rogue River Indian War of 1855-56.

• • •

This section of the Rogue River estuary supports a large variety of birds, including: cormorant, cliff swallow, great blue heron, merganser, crow, raven, common snowy egret, sea gull, turkey buzzard or vulture, kingfisher, eagle, and osprey, also called "fish hawk."

The American bald eagle is seen frequently along the Rogue River.
(Rogue River Mail Boat Trips Collection)

JOHNS HOLE

Upstream from Elephant Rock is Johns Hole, named for early day fisherman Jacob Johns.

● ● ●

The Rogue River is world famous among fishermen for chinook salmon, silver salmon, steelhead, shad, and sturgeon. Fishing guides and their parties are frequently seen on the Rogue.

● ● ●

EDSON CREEK

Avery J. Edson, who came to Oregon in the Applegate wagon train of 1846, settled on this north bank creek. Edson later married Widow Christina Giesel, a survivor of the Gold Beach Uprising on February 22, 1856. The fertile riverbank fields, called Edson Flats, were used by R.D. Hume in the early 1900s to grow peas. The peas were packed in the Hume cannery between the spring and fall salmon runs.

CANNERY RIFFLE

The Seaborg Cannery was a rival of the Macleay Estate Company (successor to R.D. Hume's company) from 1915-1919. The south bank cannery was destroyed by fire on February 20, 1927.

CLAY BANK

A twenty-five-foot brown clay bank stretches along the north side of the Rogue for about half a mile. This section of the river marks the end of tidewater, approximately four miles upstream.

FERRY RIFFLE

This riffle is at the beginning of the Ferry Hole.

FERRY HOLE

In 1866 Isaac Smith established a ferry at this deep pool on the Rogue. The William Bagnell family began running the ferry in 1876 after Smith's death, and thereafter it was locally known as Bagnell's Ferry. By 1894, a large settlement was flourishing here with a general store, salting house, several homes, and the Alaska Packers Association cannery. With the opening of the Roosevelt Highway in the 1920s, Bagnell's became an auto ferry. The public boat ramp is all that is left of the original Roosevelt Highway (now Hwy. 101), which was rerouted in 1927 causing the demise of the ferry.

Across from the Ferry Hole, the site of a former plywood mill can be seen above the gravel bar. This was the location of the February 22, 1856 Gold Beach Uprising. Among those killed were Indian Agent Ben Wright, and John Poland, leader of the Gold Beach Guards, a volunteer group of settlers. The rampaging Indians burned sixty cabins along the Rogue that night, while many pioneers fled for safety to a nearby crude stockade known as the Miners Fort.

SQUAW CREEK

An Indian woman drowned at the mouth of this creek.

CANFIELD RIFFLE

Attorney Jason W. Canfield homesteaded here in 1869. Considered a good fishing spot for salmon and steelhead, the riffle becomes quite shallow in the summer.

Doe and two fawns near the Ferry Hole.
(Rogue River Mail Boat Trips Collection)

Canfield Riffle, looking upstream.
(Authors' Photo)

JIM HUNT CREEK AND RIFFLE

James M. Hunt, a prospector of 1853, settled on this stretch of the Rogue. When the Indians had the pioneers barricaded in the Miners Fort at the mouth of the Rogue in 1856, Jim Hunt was wounded as he went outside to retrieve a cache of potatoes for the starving settlers.

SCHNEIDAU RIFFLE (WAKEMAN RIFFLE)

Gust Schneidau was a Swedish commercial fisherman who came to the Rogue River in 1924. He was a fishing guide from 1935 to 1970, and also owned a mink ranch. This riffle was originally named for James F. and Mary Elizabeth Wakeman who settled here in 1876. James Wakeman and sons built the first pole boat on the Rogue, and later James helped build the *Mary D. Hume*, a locally famous vessel that plied the waters of the Pacific from 1881 to 1978. The *Mary D.*, through an unfortunate accident, now sits partially submerged near the south end of the Rogue River Bridge, where the grand old lady of the sea awaits her final destiny.

LIBBY CREEK

David Libby settled at the mouth of this creek in 1853. He was a veteran of the Rogue River Indian War of 1855-56.

HUNTLEY PARK

Nathaniel Huntley ran the mail boat from Gold Beach to Illahe in 1901. The spring at this now private campground was Nathaniel's favorite camping spot.

BILL ASH RIFFLE

Bill Ash was a fisherman who often camped near this riffle.

KIMBALL CREEK

Ira and Amanda Kimball settled in the basin between a large hill (now Kimball Hill) and this south bank creek.

GILLESPIE RIFFLES (KIMBALL RIFFLES)

First called Kimball Riffles, this good steelhead water is now better known as Gillespie Riffles. Alexander and Thersie Gillespie arrived on the Rogue in 1873. One of their sons, Coleman, was the only man ever legally hanged in Curry County.

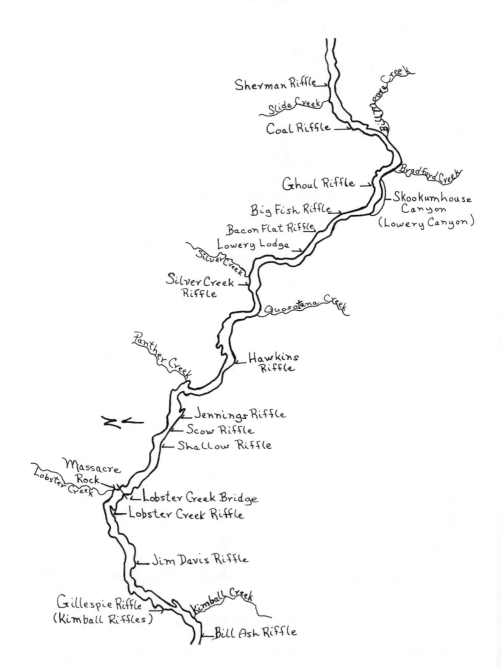

JIM DAVIS RIFFLE

Jim Davis was an early day settler.

LOBSTER CREEK RIFFLE (COFFEE RIFFLE)

Now known as Lobster Creek Riffle for the creek that enters on the north, it was called Coffee Riffle by early boatmen. They called a deep, roily hole near the north shore Devil's Coffee Pot.

LOBSTER CREEK, MASSACRE ROCK, AND LOBSTER CREEK BRIDGE

This creek was named for the freshwater crayfish, or "lobster," found here in abundance by the pioneers.

Massacre Rock is located at the mouth of the creek and is adjacent to the bridge. The rock was the site of an ambush by white settlers on two canoes of Indians in retribution for an attack on Ellensburg (Gold Beach) the night before. Unfortunately, the Indians who died were from a different group than those who attacked the town.

Lobster Creek Bridge begins the recreational section of the Rogue River. Under the Wild and Scenic Rivers Act of 1968, the recreational designation permits some development along the shoreline.

• • •

Upon leaving the Lobster Creek area, the Rogue begins to narrow, and the mountains become steeper, as the river enters the Canyon country.

The mail boat pilot is ever alert for wildlife along the Rogue, and passengers can look forward to seeing a wide variety. Common in the Rogue River Canyon are: black tailed deer; black bear (the only species found here); Roosevelt elk; cougar; bobcat; bank beaver; river otter; muskrat; Western pond turtles; and raccoon (daytime sightings of these nocturnal animals are rare).

• • •

SHALLOW RIFFLE

Upstream from Lobster Creek Bridge is Shallow Riffle, so named because it is extremely shallow in summer.

SCOW RIFFLE

Fred Lowery, mail boat pilot and son of longtime mail boat contractor Frank Lowery, kept his scow tied in this area. Fred hauled lumber and cattle, and was often helped by locally famous riverman, Ruel Hawkins.

Rogue Queen at Massacre Rock.
(Authors' Photo)

**Mail boat pilot Jim Sorber on the Wake Up Riley,
showing his passengers a bank beaver lodge.**
(Authors' Photo)

JENNINGS RIFFLE

The Jennings family had property along this stretch of the Rogue.

PANTHER CREEK

Pioneer homesteaders named this north bank creek for the numerous panther (cougar) in the area. Panthers were disliked and feared because of their ferocious attacks on settler's livestock.

DUNKLEBURGER BAR (WILLIAM MILLER RIFFLE)

This large gravel bar is a popular place for summer steelhead fishing. Dick Dunkleburger had a fishing lodge here in the 1950s. This riffle was named for William Miller, who came to the Rogue River in 1875.

HAWKINS RIFFLE

Angie Hawkins homesteaded in this area on the north bank. Her son, Ruel Hawkins, was a respected Rogue River boatman and boat mail carrier who lost his life on the Rogue in 1954.

QUOSATANA CREEK

This tributary enters the Rogue from the south and takes its name from an Indian word, *Quosaten*, meaning "clear water." There is a U.S. Forest Service campground located here.

• • •

The Rogue Canyon has a profuse assortment of trees, and mail boat passengers see many fine specimens, including: madrone, laurel, myrtle, maple, live oak, Oregon white oak, California black oak, tanoak, Port Orford cedar, Western red cedar, Douglas fir, grand fir, Western hemlock, sugar pine, ponderosa pine, Pacific yew, alder, ash, and poplar.

Shrubs, some flowering and some with fruit, found along the banks of the Rogue, are: dogwood, Western azalea, vine maple, manzanita, arrow-wood, Oregon grape, Pacific rhododendron, salal, willow, Indian potato or onion, wild Indian rhubarb or umbrella plant, wild bee vine, rasberry, blackberry, Himalaya berry, huckleberry, salmonberry, bayberry, thimble-berry, sweetbriar rose, and poison oak.

Flowers and ferns also delight the visitor to the Rogue. Found along the river and at mouths of creeks, are: golden iris, bachelor button, trillium, wild aster, Smith's fairy belle, azalea (cream or pink colored), foxglove, California fuschia, miner's lettuce, sorrel, sword fern, maidenhair fern, licorice fern, chain fern, bracken fern, lady fern, and deer fern.

The *Golden Eagle* at Hawkins Riffle.
(Rogue River Mail Boat Trips Collection)

Lowery Lodge, a famous Rogue River landmark of bygone years.
(Authors' Photo)

SILVER CREEK AND RIFFLE

Small silver colored stones found in the streambed gave this creek its name. A shallow riffle near the mouth of the north bank creek bears the same name.

ANNIE LOWERY RIFFLE

Annie Lowery was the wife of renowned mail contractor J. Frank Lowery. Annie ran "Lowery's on the Rogue," made delicious 25¢ pies, and was a favorite of the fishermen who stayed at Lowery's because she always listened with sympathetic ear to their stories of the fish that got away.

LOWERY LODGE

Located about sixteen miles upriver, this property was homesteaded in 1868 by Englishman James Lowery and his wife, Eula. Lowery's Clearing, as it was first known, supported a settlement of five or six families by 1898 and maintained a school for sixteen children. Lowery's Lodge was the overnight stop in the early years for the mail boatman, and later was the lunch stop for the mail boat, on its way to and from Agness. "Lowery's on the Rogue" became a famous fishing lodge, and was run by the family until 1959. Like sad eyes, the empty windows of the abandoned old lodge watch today's mail boats as if remembering the glory of former days.

BACON FLAT RIFFLE

Pioneer Charles Davis was the first on the river to cure bacon. Riverfolk called his homestead "Bacon Flat" for the wonderful aroma along this stretch of the Rogue.

BIG FISH RIFFLE

Mail boat driver Fred Lowery caught an extremely large salmon in this riffle.

SKOOKUMHOUSE CANYON (LOWERY CANYON)

Originally called Lowery Canyon for 1868 settler Jim Lowery, the canyon is now better known for Skookumhouse Butte which towers over the Rogue on the south.

SKOOKUMHOUSE BUTTE

Rising 2,191 feet above the Rogue, the butte was the site of an Indian fortress built to protect them from the encroaching white settlers. Taken from the Chinook Jargon word *skookum,* meaning "strong," and combined with "house," *skookumhouse* meant "stronghouse" or "strong-fort."

GHOUL RIFFLE (FRY'S LANDING)

The Rogue River shifts this shallow riffle from north to south each year during the winter high water. It was named for the Gould family, who were summer residents, but slowly through the years vocal inflection changed it to its present "spirited" name. In the early days, this area was called Fry's Landing for one of the many branches of the Fry family who lived here.

BRADFORD CREEK

A man named Bradford and his two wives settled by this creek.

BILL MOORE CREEK (PULLIAM PLACE)

William Moore, a veteran of the Rogue River Indian War of 1855-56, settled here in 1887. Moore farmed and was also a commercial fisherman. In the 1930s, the Pulliam family came each summer to the Rogue to fish. Their home was washed away in the 1964 flood.

COAL RIFFLE

The *Gold Beach Gazette* on January 26, 1894 reported: "Postmaster Charles (Dewey) yesterday laid in his winter's supply of coal. He picked up on the beach a large chunk of fine coal, which the river floods brought down from the coal veins up the river. The coal up the river is a superior article, and should be opened up and placed on the market." Around 1900, a boat loaded with coal from an upriver mine capsized here, and both boat and coal were lost. Unfortunately, the accident also caused the closure of the coal mine.

SLIDE CREEK AND RIFFLE

This north bank creek and riffle are named for the huge mud and rock slide that occurred at its headwaters. The scenic section of the Rogue begins at Slide Creek. The Wild and Scenic Rivers Act of 1968 designates the scenic stretch to be essentially undeveloped, but may be accessible in places by roads.

• • •

Sightings of osprey, sometimes referred to as "fish hawk," are common along the river. Mail boat pilot Stan Wade estimates there are up to eighty osprey nests in the Rogue River Canyon, but fourteen years ago, Stan recalls, mail boat passengers were extremely lucky to see ten osprey nests. Today's large osprey population gives the river visitor a chance to see these birds up close in their natural habitat.

The latin name for osprey is *pandion haliaetus*. In Greek mythology, Pandion was king of Athens. His two daughters and their husband were turned into birds. *Haliaetus* is the Greek word for "eagle that hunts the sea." The osprey is the only species in its family.

The mature osprey has a wing span of up to six feet. They mate for life, returning each year from their migration to Mexico and Central America to the same nest, rebuilding or adding on as necessary.

Osprey usually lay three eggs; the colors range from white to cinnamon brown, daubed with chocolate brown. The male osprey supplies all the fish for the chicks, and the female breaks up the fish for the young until they are five or six weeks old. After the sixth week, the chicks sit on the fish, while using their talons to feed themselves.

The osprey usually leave the Rogue River Canyon for their southern migration in late September. Riverfolk expect a cold winter in the years the osprey leave early.

• • •

SHERMAN RIFFLE

The Sherman family homesteaded on the Rogue River in this area.

WAKE UP RILEY CREEK

The quaint name of this creek comes from an often told tragic tale of the search for the elusive metal—gold. Around 1870, Judge Riley and five fellow prospectors came to this creek following rumors of gold. Weeks of panning and searching yielded only a few flakes, so the men decided to leave. On their last morning, one gold seeker woke before the others and went to the stream one final time. It was his lucky day for he found the rumored deposit and quickly ran back to camp yelling, "Wake up Riley. Wake Up Riley. We've struck it rich!" But the end had come for Judge Riley, who had died in his sleep and never knew of the good fortune.

RACHEL'S DELIGHT

Many years ago a young Englishwoman and her father came to the Rogue on a fishing trip. Rachel caught several chinook salmon at this riffle, and, so the story goes, each time she caught a fish, she exclaimed, "Isn't this delightful!"

The osprey return to the same nest every year.
(Rogue River Mail Boat Trips Collection)

The gliding river near Sherman Riffle.
(Authors' Photo)

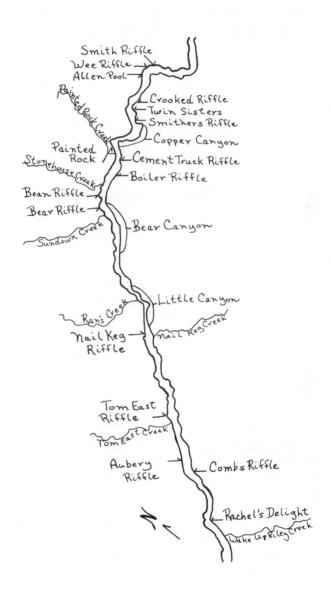

COMBS RIFFLE

E.E. Combs built a lodge and several guest houses overlooking this riffle. The Combs lodge washed away in the 1964 flood, and mail boat pilot Gary Combs remembers watching his grandfather's home float under the Rogue River Bridge and out into the Pacific.

AUBERY RIFFLE

Rogue River settler Amaziah Aubery became the first postmaster of Agness.

TOM EAST CREEK AND RIFFLE

Tommy East was an old-time prospector and volunteer "mailman" in the days before the mail boat service. The homestead of pioneers John and Sadie Adams, called Potato Illahe Ranch, was located here on the north bank of the Rogue about twenty-five miles from Gold Beach. Scott Adams, their great-grandson, is currently a mail boat pilot.

NAIL KEG CREEK AND RIFFLE

A cask of nails came round the horn through hazardous waters and gales to the Rogue River, an isolated country where nails were rarer and more precious than gold. An Indian squaw had the keg in a canoe and was paddling upstream near the mouth of this creek, when the swift current caught her. The squaw, the canoe, and the nails were lost to the Rogue.

LITTLE CANYON

This canyon is the narrowest section of the Rogue River below Agness. During the 1964 flood, the river rose about 100 feet here and scoured all the plants and trees from the canyon walls. Mail boat passengers often see river otter frolicking in the shallow water along the shore in Little Canyon.

RAN'S CREEK

Through the years this stream has also been called Bridge Creek and Tiger Creek. The stream is now named for Randolph T. Meservey, who was a mail boat pilot, river freighter, commercial fisherman, and later a fishing guide for "Lowery's on the Rogue."

NEW RIFFLE

This riffle was formed in recent years.

BEAR CANYON

The mail boat pilots named the canyon for the many black bear that are seen here.

SUNDOWN CREEK

A group of men reached this stream at sundown and camped overnight on its banks. Today many of the mail boat drivers call this Rhubarb Creek for the Indian rhubarb, or umbrella plant, growing at its mouth.

BEAR RIFFLE

Located at the top end of Bear Canyon, this riffle is named for the black bear that commonly prowl the banks here.

BEAN RIFFLE

A riverboat loaded with beans upset in this riffle.

STONEHOUSE CREEK

This north bank stream is named for the nearby stone ledge that Indians and early travelers used for shelter.

BOILER RIFFLE

The steamer *Rogue River*, specially designed and built at Portland in 1900 to run on the Rogue, sank near this riffle in 1902, loaded with twenty-five tons of cargo. Only the ship's boiler remained, and it finally washed away many years later in the '64 flood.

CEMENT TRUCK RIFFLE

A cement truck was sitting in the middle of the Illinois River Bridge when the flood waters of 1964 washed it downriver and deposited it on this gravel bar. For many years, the truck had a sign that read, "We deliver anywhere."

PAINTED ROCK AND PAINTED ROCK CREEK

The natural colors of this riverside monolith may have suggested its name. It was the site of an Indian village, and legend has it that the rock was used as a message center for travelers on the river. The last battle of the Rogue River Indian War took place here on June 6, 1856. The Indians killed in the fight were those who had refused to surrender.

Little Canyon, the narrowest point on the Rogue below Agness.
(Authors' Photo)

Black bear are often seen in Bear Canyon.
(Rogue River Mail Boat Trips Collection)

COPPER CANYON

Sheer cliffs rise 400 feet above the Rogue in this canyon, which takes its name from the copper colored rock walls. In past floods, the Rogue has risen as much as 110 feet in Copper Canyon. Even in summer, the river reaches a depth of sixty feet, and is a good refuge for Rogue River sturgeon.

• • •

Sturgeon belong to an ancient group of fish. They are long, bony, and slow growing—a six-foot fish may be 100 years old. When full-grown they can weigh as much as 1,000 pounds and reach a length of twenty feet. Sturgeon mature late and do not begin reproducing until they are fifteen years of age. Conservation efforts impose strict fishing regulations for this rare species.

• • •

SMITHERS RIFFLE

D.B. Smithers came to the Rogue in 1932 and homesteaded above this riffle. In the early years he grew grapefruit, lemons, oranges, and figs on his rich land.

TWIN SISTERS

Two identical rocks located in the river give this area its name.

CROOKED RIFFLE

Historically this has been one of the most difficult riffles on the Rogue to navigate because of its sharp right angle turn. In the early 1900s, the *Copper Queen*, a ninety-foot steam vessel, tried to reach Agness heavily loaded with miner's supplies. She was stopped short of her destination because she could not negotiate the 90° bend at Crooked Riffle.

ALLEN POOL

Allen Pool is known for good steelhead fishing.

WEE RIFFLE

This small narrow riffle, with rocks strewn about under the surface, was once called Lower Smith Riffle by Rogue boatmen.

SMITH RIFFLE

The Smith family settled along this stretch of the Rogue.

Twin Sisters, looking upstream.
(Authors' Photo)

The *Rogue* at Crooked Riffle.
(Rogue River Mail Boat Trips Collection)

HOTEL RIFFLE

A good fishing spot, named by vacationing fishermen for the old Agness Hotel.

HOG EDDY

A boatload of hogs was lost here in front of the Lucas' dock.

LUCAS PIONEER RANCH

John Day and S.E. "Lizzie" Cooley homesteaded the original 200-acre site of today's Lucas Pioneer Ranch. After some years, John and Lizzie established the Cooley Hotel. In 1916 their daughter, Sadie Lucas, built the Agness Hotel. Larry Lucas, son of Sadie Lucas Pettinger, became the sole owner of Lucas Pioneer Ranch in the 1930s. Today the lodge is owned by Larry's five children and managed by his son Willard Lucas.

Lucas Pioneer Ranch is noted for its family-style dinners, featuring corn-on-the-cob grown on the ranch, and is one of three lunch stops for mail boat passengers. Guests are encouraged to walk freely about the lodge grounds, where they will find interesting artifacts from earlier years.

The mail boat truck at Lucas Pioneer Ranch landing.
(Authors' Photo)

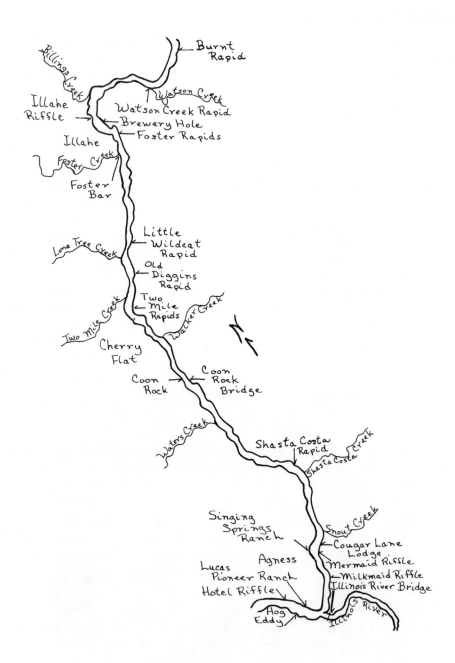

ILLINOIS RIVER AND BRIDGE

The largest of the Rogue's tributaries, the Illinois River, was named by three brothers, Samuel, John, and Phillip Althouse, who were early day placer miners on the upper river. The Althouse brothers left Peoria, Illinois and came to Oregon in 1847.

The December 1964 flood washed out the nearly completed Illinois River Bridge. The existing bridge was built at the same place, but twenty feet higher. At the confluence of the Illinois, the upstream course of the Rogue River heads north until it reaches Big Bend, where it resumes a northeasterly course toward Blossom Bar.

AGNESS

The town of Agness is thirty-two miles upriver from Gold Beach and marks the turnaround point for the 64-mile mail boat trip. The community stretches along both sides of the river from Lucas Pioneer Ranch past Singing Springs Ranch to Cougar Lane Lodge. The settlement's first postmaster was Amaziah Aubery, who named the post office for his daughter, Agnes, but somehow in 1897 the Post Office Department added an extra "s." Today Agness has a post office, a one-room schoolhouse, community center, library, and three resorts, all lunch stops for the mail boat trips. And, according to current postmaster Sandy Stallard, the Agness area, including Illahe, has a population of 150.

AGNESS SUSPENSION BRIDGE

The concrete pylon on the west bank, and some twisted steel down-river, are all that remain of the Forest Service bridge that was swept away in the 1964 flood. The bridge had been brought upriver piece by piece in the Carter-Miller mail boats for an Oregon City firm, Clackamas Construction Company, and dedicated on April 21, 1932. Through a similarity of initials—"CCC"—the bridge construction has sometimes been attributed to the Civilian Conservation Corps, but the Agness CCC camp was not established until a year after the bridge was completed.

MILKMAID RIFFLE

This riffle was named for a pretty Indian maiden who milked her cow along this stretch of the river.

SINGING SPRINGS RANCH

Built in 1951 by B.W. and Lynn Griffitts on forty acres, the resort is named for the springs that bubble out of the hillside below the restaurant. Singing Springs Ranch was purchased in 1965 by Ted Blokker. He sold it in 1969 to Rudy and Dolores Valente. Since 1987 the resort has been operated by Bill and Julie Scherbarth, and in 1988 they were joined by Bill's brother, John, and his wife, Gemma.

The Scherbarths provide a friendly relaxed atmosphere, while serving a wide variety of delicious meals. Singing Springs Ranch is popular with mail boat passengers who enjoy lunch on a spacious deck overlooking the Rogue River, while seated at tables covered with the Singing Springs' trademark, aqua and white umbrellas.

**Stan Wade talks to his passengers before leaving the
Singing Springs dock at Agness on the 104-mile whitewater trip.
U. S. Coast Guard regulations require life jackets to be worn through the rapids.**
(Authors' Photo)

MERMAID ROCK AND RIFFLE

Indian legend tells us that in the long ago time on the Rogue, young braves proved their love for their maidens by swimming the river at this point in winter, when the water was the highest, swiftest, and coldest. On one occasion, the story goes, a handsome warrior lost his life in the river while trying to cross to his love. For many years afterward, the pretty, young heartbroken Indian maid would go down to a large rock at the river's edge, where she would sing softly, while waving her arms gracefully, waiting for her lost suitor to emerge from the Rogue. It is said that through the years her gently haunting song has led many fishermen to their deaths as they tried to reach the beautiful vision they thought was a mermaid.

COUGAR LANE LODGE

The original Cougar Lane store was built in 1949 at the corner of Cougar Lane and Rattlesnake Avenue in "downtown" Agness, under the world famous "Heidelberg tree." Each year the myrtle tree was decorated at Christmas with Heidelberg cans, and it was also a favorite gathering place in the summer. Bernard and Clarice Jackson purchased the Cougar Lane store in 1957.

After twenty-one years in Agness, the Jacksons built a lodge on the opposite bank of the Rogue in East Agness, and moved their popular store to the new location in April 1978. Cougar Lane Lodge offers a motel, gas station, grocery store, boat dock and ramp, RV campground, and restaurant with adjacent bar. Passengers on either the 64-mile or 80-mile boat trip may enjoy their lunch break at this rustic lodge.

SNOUT CREEK

This creek enters the Rogue on the east bank and was named for a dog. Snout was a good tracker and one time while out rounding up some straying cattle, he became ill. The little dog died beside the creek that now bears his name.

SHASTA COSTA RAPID AND CREEK

The *Shistakoostee* band lived in this area of the Rogue, and in 1854 they numbered around 145. Shasta Costa Rapid is the first rapid on the 80-mile and 104-mile whitewater mail boat trips. The summer of 1977 was a low water year and sand bags were used at this point to deepen the river channel.

WATERS CREEK

Miner George M. Waters lived near the mouth of this creek at the turn of the century.

COON ROCK BRIDGE

Coon Rock Bridge across the Rogue River was completed in 1962. Two years later the bridge was tested when it was inundated by the floodwaters of the rampaging Rogue. It survived, although the river flowed over the top. Coon Rock is located on the west bank just upstream from the bridge.

WALKER CREEK

Antone Walker, a Portugese sailor, came to the Rogue in 1880, where he first chose land on Mule Creek and later moved to the Cherry Flat area. After a hugging match with a bear when his gun misfired, Tony Walker gained local fame as the "one-eared bear-fighter."

CHERRY FLAT

Located on a big bench along the west bank of the Rogue, Cherry Flat has long been popular with river folk for its fertile soil. The *Gold Beach Globe* on April 1, 1913 reported news about a Cherry Flat resident: "Agness—Our friend and neighbor C.D. Cunningham has put one over on Luther Burbank, the plant wizard, by successfully grafting a cherry tree onto an elderberry stock. But—Oh, what will the harvest be!"

TWO MILE RAPIDS AND CREEK

Two Mile Rapids is named for its distance from Agness and is one of the more exciting and rough rapids. The rapids is long and steep, creating a thrilling whitewater experience for the mail boat passengers. A large Indian settlement was sited along the gravel bar near the mouth of Two Mile Creek, located just upstream from the rapids. There are petroglyphs on some of the large boulders in this area, and artifacts have been found that date back 1,500 to 2,000 years. Visitors can see an example of the petroglyphs of this area at the Curry County Museum in Gold Beach.

OLD DIGGINS RAPID

Around 1900, miners dammed the Rogue's main channel and diverted the river to the west side of the island in order to expose the natural rock "sluice boxes." The miners then recovered the gold that had accumulated in the rocks through the years. The floodwaters of the Rogue washed the low rock diversion dam out the following winter.

LONE TREE CREEK

This stream was named for a large, lone, lightning-scarred tree near its headwaters.

LITTLE WILDCAT RAPID

This whitewater area has characteristics similar to Wildcat Rapid, which is located above Blossom Bar. Little Wildcat Rapid is marked by a sharp turn in the channel of the river. Skill is needed to safely navigate between large rocks just under the surface of the water at the top of the rapid.

FOSTER BAR AND CREEK

The large gravel bar here is a major take-out point for the downriver float trips. This is the first road access for the rafters and drift boats, whose trip begins forty miles up the Rogue. The Rogue River Trail, popular with hikers, parallels the river from Grave Creek Landing to Big Bend pasture. The gravel bar and upstream creek are named for Charles Foster, captain in the Gold Beach Guards, who homesteaded near the mouth of the creek. After the Rogue River Indian War ended, Charley was a miner, packer, farmer, and occasional hunting guide.

ILLAHE

The name of the first upriver post office and this community is taken from the Indian word *ilahekh*, meaning "beautiful land." The renowned George Washington Meservey was postmaster here from 1918 to 1940, and was succeeded by his wife Rose, who served until the Illahe and Agness post offices were merged in 1943.

FOSTER RAPIDS

Named for Charles Foster, who homesteaded nearby, this is a long rapid full of rocks and whitewater. The upper end of Foster Rapids is extremely narrow during low water periods.

BIG BEND

At the beginning of this lengthy curve in the river, the Rogue resumes its northeasterly course.

The last major battle of the Rogue River Indian War of 1855-56 took place in a long meadow on the north side. Several well-known river families have lived at Big Bend over the years, including Jake and Yreka Fry, the original homesteaders. Will and Susie White established their Hunter's Lodge here; and Charles and Sadie Lucas Pettinger called this place the Big Bend Ranch. Charlie Pettinger had the upriver pack train mail contract from Agness to Marial and used this pasture for his mules. The Big Bend Ranch house burned down on July 14, 1959.

Elijah Price, father of the mail boats, homesteaded across the Rogue, and his log cabin was the first Illahe post office in 1895.

BREWERY HOLE

Located in the Big Bend area, Brewery Hole was named in the 1960s for the river foam, or "suds," which are often seen along this stretch of the Rogue.

ILLAHE LODGE

Built in 1944 by Ernest J. and Florence Schneider, the Illahe Lodge has long been a favorite fishing and vacation retreat along the river. Construction materials for the lodge were brought upstream by the mail boats. Illahe Lodge is owned by the Schneider's daughter, Carolyn Rutledge, and managed by her son and daughter-in-law, Ernie and Violet Rutledge.

ILLAHE RIFFLE

Illahe Riffle is probably one of the shallowest areas of the Rogue to navigate. The channel on the south side of the river is impassable because of solid bedrock, so the mail boats are forced to use the narrow north side channel, which averages less than twelve inches of water during the summer.

BILLINGS CREEK

In 1882 John Billings had a grist mill 200 yards up this creek, where settlers in the area brought their corn and wheat for grinding.

WATSON CREEK AND RAPID

Hunter-trapper George Watson built his cabin just to the east of the south bank creek that bears his name. Watson Creek Rapid is the turn-around point for the 80-mile whitewater mail boat trip. The return trip includes a stop at Agness for lunch, or dinner on the afternoon trip, before heading downstream to the mouth of the Rogue. Watson Creek Rapid is also the beginning of the wild section of the Rogue River. Under the Wild and Scenic Rivers Act of 1968, the wild section of the Rogue is preserved in a natural, wild, and primitive condition unaltered by the effects of man.

BURNT RAPID

This small rapid is named for the area's black colored rocks, which were charred by a forest fire. The fire burned to the water's edge and then jumped the Rogue at this point before finally being controlled. In summer low water, it is possible to see submerged boulders or slabs of bedrock through the clear river water. Burnt Rapid is at the top end of Big Bend as the mail boat continues upstream.

DAN'S CREEK

The creek on the north bank was named for Indian Dan, who homesteaded here in the 1860s.

MASON'S WALL

The large, square stones along the Rogue's edge at this point appear to be a man-made mortared landing, but the blackish-rocks have been precisely segmented by the natural action of the water.

HICK'S CREEK

Hick Meservey, son of Illahe postmaster George Washington Meservey, was an accomplished riverman who freighted supplies on the Rogue.

PEYTON RAPIDS

Jim Peyton homesteaded along the Rogue's south bank. A long whitewater area, Peyton Rapids has many large rocks under the surface which make it a challenge to navigate.

FLEA CREEK

Flea Creek, entering the Rogue on the north, was named by pioneers because it was no bigger than a flea. And on the bank opposite Flea Creek is a rivulet so small it has no name.

FLORA DELL CREEK

This creek was named for a young girl, Flora Dell Thomas. She married packer and mail carrier Hathaway Jones, who earned fame along the Rogue River Canyon as a teller of tall tales. Flora Dell Creek has a beautiful waterfall that drops about 200 feet to a deep pool before entering the Rogue River.

CLAY HILL STILLWATER

A two-to-three-mile stretch of calm, perfectly flat water, Clay Hill Stillwater is one of the most peaceful areas along the Rogue.

CLAY HILL RAPIDS

The clay-colored hill on the north side of the Rogue gives this area its name. Clay Hill Rapids, the second steepest on the lower Rogue, must be navigated in two steps because of the sharp right angle bend in the channel. The large passenger mail boats going up or downstream stop in the eddy between the two whitewater areas so the pilot can reposition the blue hydrojet before picking up speed to run the remaining section of the rapids.

CLAY HILL LODGE

Marked by a curving sand beach and a strangely shaped ponderosa pine called the "Dinosaur Tree," Clay Hill Lodge is the lunch stop for the mail boat company's 104-mile wilderness trip. Rooms are available for those who might want to stay longer.

Originally the homestead of George Thomas, the lodge was purchased in 1943 by Tom Staley, Sr. and is now leased from the Staley family by Larry and Clare Bowen. The Bowens have kept the flavor of a true wilderness lodge by leaving the grounds in a natural state. Guests enjoy a magnificent view of the Rogue from the two-story lodge and deck area while partaking of a tasty lunch. The hour-and-a-half lunch break allows the visitor time to cross Clay Hill Creek on a wooden bridge and walk part way up the Rogue River Trail, or sit quietly beside the water on the curving sandy beach. The cabin of the original homestead is a short walk and can be easily reached.

CAMP TACOMA RAPIDS

Named by a family from Tacoma, Washington who camped here to mine for gold, Camp Tacoma Rapids is a rocky whitewater area upstream from Clay Hill Lodge.

TATE CREEK

An early day prospector, "Doc" Tate, who died before 1894, is buried at the mouth of this creek.

SOLITUDE BAR AND RAPIDS

The Solitude Mining Company worked this area around 1900, and tailings (piles of rocks from mining days) can still be found above the Rogue River Trail. For author Zane Grey, Solitude Bar was a favorite camping, fishing, and writing site. He described Solitude as a "clean, lonely, sweet-smelling place, with the gliding river below; and across it the green-and-yellow timbered mountain rising splendidly, with gray crags touching the skies." The author wrote much of his famous *Rogue River Feud* while spending a summer at Solitude Bar.

BRUSHY BAR

In 1856 Indians ambushed Capt. William Tichenor and his men by rolling rocks down the steep hillside onto them, after which the area became known as Tichenor's Defeat. Miner and volunteer mail carrier Tommy East settled here in 1880. East built a cabin, and continued to travel his yearly prospecting route until 1897, when he died at eighty-seven years

Stan Wade gunning through Clay Hill Rapids.
(Rogue River Mail Boat Trips Collection)

Looking downriver from Clay Hill Lodge.
(Authors' Photo)

of age. The turn of the century found a large hydraulic mining operation on this gravel bar, and in 1905 a forest fire which burned all summer gave this area its current name, for only low dense brush grew back on the bar following the fire.

EAST CREEK

On the south bank across from Brushy Bar is a creek named for miner Tommy East. The bluff above East Creek was the site of the Eagles Nest, vacation retreat of Generals Ira Eaker, Carl Spaatz, Fred Anderson, Nathan Twining, and Curtis LeMay. All that remains are the stairs and a chimney.

HUGGINS CANYON

The north cliff towers 1,000 feet over the mighty Rogue in this canyon named for miner-trapper Andy Huggins, who lived upstream at Half Moon Bar. The most dramatic gorge on the Rogue, Huggins Canyon is home to eagles that nest along the rugged ridge of Devil's Backbone, and sturgeon lurking in a midcanyon pool seventy feet deep. Sheer canyon walls seem to hug the mail boat, wrapping passengers in a cocoon of isolation and beauty, dwarfing the craft as it glides smoothly through dark-green water.

QUARTER INCH RAPID

Quarter Inch Rapid is an extremely narrow, short whitewater area named by passenger boat pilots who claimed there was only a quarter inch clearance on each side of the boat as it passed between two rocks in the rapid. Measurements later confirmed that there was at least half an inch on both sides.

HALF MOON BAR AND RAPIDS

Named for the half-moon shaped bend in the river's channel, Half Moon Bar was the site of miner-trapper Andy Huggins' homestead. The rapids consist of three distinct areas and provide an exciting whitewater adventure.

PARADISE BAR

Paradise Bar is an elevated bench that runs parallel to a long stretch of river with riffles at the lower and upper ends. Charlie Pettinger home-steaded here before moving on to Big Bend and securing the Agness-to-Marial pack mule mail contract.

Camp Tacoma Rapids.
(Authors' Photo)

Huggins Canyon.
(Authors' Photo)

Looking down Devil's Staircase Rapids, where the river climbs 30 feet in 300 yards.
(Authors' Photo)

Boulder-choked Blossom Bar is the end of navigation for powerboats.
(Authors' Photo)

PARADISE CREEK

This creek cascades over a rock on the north bank before frothily entering the Rogue. It was named by a gold prospector who thought he had reached "Paradise" when he came upon this lovely stream and waterfall.

DEVIL'S STAIRCASE RAPIDS

An exciting whitewater area, Devil's Staircase Rapids is the steepest on the 104-mile wilderness trip. It is named for the rough whitewater waves leading to the top of the rapids. Devil's Staircase is also the last upstream rapid navigable by hydrojet.

BLOSSOM BAR RAPIDS

Named by pioneers for the wild azaleas growing along the banks, Blossom Bar was home to an Indian village along the north bank, and later was the site of a stamp mill used to process gold ore. Blossom Bar is a long, steep stretch of whitewater choked with huge boulders. When writer Zane Grey first saw it, he said Blossom Bar should have been called "Boulder Bar." From this section upstream, the Rogue is not navigable by powerboat or hyrdojet, although rafts and drift boats float downstream from Grave Creek Landing and maneuver through Blossom Bar.

The mail boat has come fifty-two miles up the Rogue and will now return downriver to Clay Hill Lodge for lunch. The journey is but half over; more whitewater, wildlife, and spectacular scenery await the mail boat passengers on the downstream trip through the magnificent Rogue River Canyon, while making the entire experience truly memorable.

● ● ●

WHAT THE MAIL BOAT PASSENGERS SAY...

People from every state and province in North America, and from over fifty other countries, have taken mail boat trips up the Rogue River. Here are some comments from the guest books:

** "It's a trip we'll always remember, and a story that will be told many times." (Kansas)

** "Most fun I've had in ages!" (Illinois)

** "Great trip, great river, great wildlife." (Germany)

** "An excellent adventure!" (California)

** "Wonderful experience, I'll be back." (Arizona)

** "I will always remember the wonderful Rogue River." (Japan)

** "An experience of a lifetime!" (Virginia)

** "GREETINGS FRIENDS! BEAUTIFUL TRIP!" (Written in Russian) (USSR)

** "Absolutely marvelous—I'll tell Iowa!" (Iowa)

** "High point of our Western vacation." (Ohio)

** "5 bear, 20 deer, 2 eagles, 6 otters—Excellent." (Canada)

** "Wonderful romp with nature and the river." (England)

** "Fantastic—like riding through a picture!" (Texas)

** "Exhilarating—made me happy!" (Georgia)

** "Fantastic trip up the river with Stan—a high point of our travels in U.S." (Austria)

ROGUE RIVER MAIL BOAT TRIPS
P.O. Box 1165
Gold Beach, OR 97444
Call (503) 247-7033

A Parting Glance...

And that is the story of the Rogue River mail boats, a phenomenon of American ingenuity and enterprise. Born of necessity and pledged to service, the proud boats of the mail fleet have been and are much like the famous river they travel: always changing, yet the same; familiar, yet new.

Such, too, can be said of the able boatmen who have guided them in the past and who guide them now; faces and names emerging, fading, changing. Yet they are somehow the same, these mail boatmen, imbued with a like spirit and care for the river, the boats, and the wildlife. They are unique as a group, set apart. And they are all a joy to ride with.

For each individual passenger, a trip up the Rogue River in a mail boat is a journey of discovery into the past as well as the present, educational as well as entertaining. And for each, the lore of the Rogue comes to life in the names of the riffles and rapids, the creeks and landmarks, recalling early years on the river, and the miners and settlers who lived their lives in splendid, isolated beauty.

The story in this book must remain an unfinished saga. For with all the tens of thousands of people who have marveled at the wonders of the Rogue from a mail boat, there will be tens of thousands more to come, and more after that. They will come, they will see, they will experience and be refreshed.

And they will never forget.

Notes On Sources

There have been no prior books written solely on the Rogue River mail boats, and, surprisingly, rather little has been done even in a general way on the history of the Agness-Illahe area for the period from 1890 to 1950. Henry Teller Price, son of Elijah Price, wrote and self-published a brief monograph in 1967, entitled *Up the Rogue River and the First Mail Route*, that has some value. Florence Arman's *The Rogue: A River to Run* (1982) and Kay Atwood's *Illahe* (1978) contain interesting Rogue River lore, though neither provides information, beyond brief references, on the mail boats.

Emil Peterson's and Alfred Powers' *A Century of Coos and Curry* (1952) and Lewis A. McArthur's *Oregon Geographic Names* (1982 ed.) have information on lower Rogue River landmarks, and the Peterson-Powers book makes several brief references to the mail boats.

The Curry County Historical Society provided some valuable material on upriver personalities through detailed articles published in their periodical, *Curry County Echoes*. Particularly helpful were the recollections of Ella Price Macfarlane and the many excellent profiles written by Walt Schroeder.

Also of assistance were back issues of the publications of the Oregon Postal History Society: the *Oregon Postal History Journal* and the earlier *The Postal Historian*. Especially informative were the recollections of Sadie Lucas Pettinger and pieces on Stuart X and Stanley Anderson.

• • •

The chief reliance in the research and preparation of this book, however, was on primary sources—newspapers of the day, records of the Post Office Department, and interviews with former mail boat contractors and pilots, as well as interviews with longtime upriver residents.

As secondary resources, interviews were conducted with descendants of early-century mail boatmen, and a myriad of national magazine pieces were perused for information.

In addition, Gary Combs and Ed and Sue Kammer loaned thick scrapbooks of clippings from periodicals, newsletters, and out-of-state newspapers relating to the Rogue River mail boats.

Unfortunately, almost all of the mail boat company records prior to 1964 were lost in the great flood.

Index